PROBLEMS AND POSSIBILITIES OF THE US ECONOMY

Marc Stoffers

Rev. date: 09/30/2020

To order additional copies of this book, contact:
Xlibris
844-714-8691
www.Xlibris.com
Orders@Xlibris.com
819722

Contents

1 Introduction vii

2 Balance of Payment...1
    2A Imports... 1
    2B Exports 5
    2C Trade Balance 10

3 Impact of Market Loss on GDP 12
    3A Impact on GDP by sector 14

4 Labor Market...16

5 Government Budget... 20

6 Conclusions Regarding Market Loss 22

7 Improvement Economic Performance....................23
    7A Investing in skills... 23
    7B Promote a level playing field with regard to foreign
    trade partners.. 24
    7C Winning the race by a robust innovation system..................... 28

8 Policy Options to Improve Economic Performance 47
    8A Stimulating investments by lowering taxes and
    increasing net profits... 47
    8B Improving scores regarding institutions...................... 49
    8C Reducing inequality by improving primary and
    secondary education... 50
    8D Improving competitiveness by stimulating STEM at
    tertiary education... 52

8E Improving competitiveness by increasing energy productivity. *54*
*8F Agencies can play an important part in the knowledge
economy*... *60*

9 Summary...63

A description of the economic development during 2000-2016, weak and strong points of the US economy and some policy recommendations.

1 INTRODUCTION

The economic crisis in 2008 has hit the US economy very hard. After a period of a GDP growth of 2,5 % per annum during 2000-2007, the US economy went into a deep depression in 2008 and 2009. From 2010 a recovery took place, which was stimulated by the financial stabilization and fiscal stimulus policies starting in late 2008 and early 2009. Nevertheless the growth of GDP dropped to an average of 1,3 % per annum in the period 2007-2016.These developments also had an impact on the labor market. As a result of weak demand for labor the unemployment rate rose from 4,6 % in 2007 to 9,3 % in 2009. After 2010 this percentage gradually declined to 4,9 % in 2016. However this figure does not take into account discouraged workers who are not actively looking for a job and are not incorporated in labor supply. So the "real" unemployment rate could be much higher. Owing to the less favorable situation on the labor market there was a stagnation of wages. The deficit on the current account went from 3,9 % of GDP in 2000 to 5,8 % in 2006 and declined gradually to 2,3 % in 2016. During 2002-2016 government expenditures exceeded revenues, which implied an continuing deficit.

Graph 1: GDP Growth, Unemployment Rate, Current Account Deficit And Government Deficit

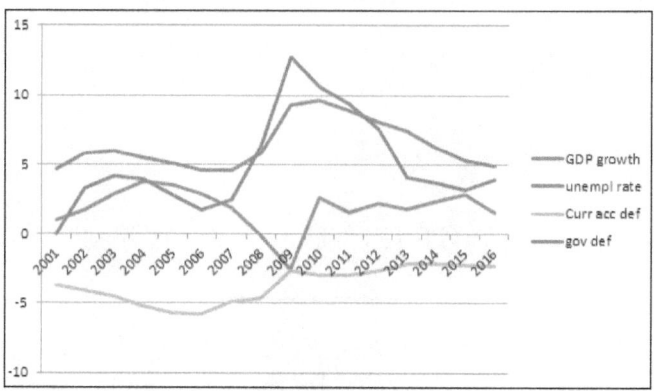

Source IMF database

In the next chapters we will discuss the above mentioned main issues of the US economy: the balance of payment, the labor market and the government budget. In addition the impact of market losses on GDP will be described as well as some measures to improve the economic performance of the US. A lot of attention will be paid to the innovation system, using information from the Global Innovation Index (GII). Then a summary will be presented.

2 BALANCE OF PAYMENT

2A Imports

Total imports amounted to 2718 billion dollar in 2016, which can be divided in 81 % goods and 19% services. Table 1 shows the composition of the imported goods by category in 2016.

Table 1: Composition of imported goods (%) in 2016

Foods, Feeds Etc.	5,9
Crude Oil, Oil Products	6,7
Industrial Supplies	13,5
Capital Goods	27
Automotive Vehicles	16
Consumer Goods	26,6
Other Goods	4,3

Source : US Census Bureau

Capital goods, consumer goods, industrial supplies (including crude oil and oil products), automotive vehicles are the main import categories. The most important partners with regard to imports are China, the European Union, Canada, Mexico, Japan and South Korea. Demand for imports depends on final demand (Private consumption, Government consumption, Gross capital formation and Exports). Using an input output table for the US of 2000[1] a Cumulative Production Structure (CPS) matrix

---

[1] Based on the make, use and import matrix from the BEA.

can be calculated, which links final demand to primary inputs (imports, labor costs, capital costs, taxes).[2] In the case of imports not only the direct imports are calculated, but also the indirect imports for the intermediary production.

Table 2 Shows that private consumption is the most important final demand category for imports followed by gross capital formation, exports and government consumption. No less than 53 % of imports is determined by private consumption.

Table 2: Calculation Import Volume On The Basis Of
Final Demand And The Realization Of Imports.

	Private Cons.	Government Cons.	Investments	Exports	Total
Share(a)	0,53	0,05	0,28	0,14	1,00
Annual volume growth 2000-2016 in % (b)	2,2	1	1	3,4	
Contribution=a*b	1,17	0,05	0,28	0,49	2,0
Realization import volume growth 2000-2016					3,1
Realization import volume growth excl. crude oil					3,8

Annual import growth during the period 2000-2016 exceeds the import growth which can be calculated from final demand. This means that the share of domestic production has declined. Foreign production has superseded US production. The loss of market share is even larger when imports are corrected for crude oil and oil products.[3]

---

[2] In matrix terms CPS =P*((1-A)^-1))*F +W, where P=matrix of primary input coefficients, A=matrix of input output coefficients of intermediary deliveries, F=matrix of final demand from domestic production,((1-A)^-1))*F=gross production and W=matrix of direct primary inputs to final demand.

[3] For a good analysis it is better to correct for oil because the oil market has its own dynamics such as the increase of domestic oil production during the reference period which has dampened total imports

Graph 2 Total Import Volume, Import Volume Corrected For Oil And Calculated Import From A CPS Matrix

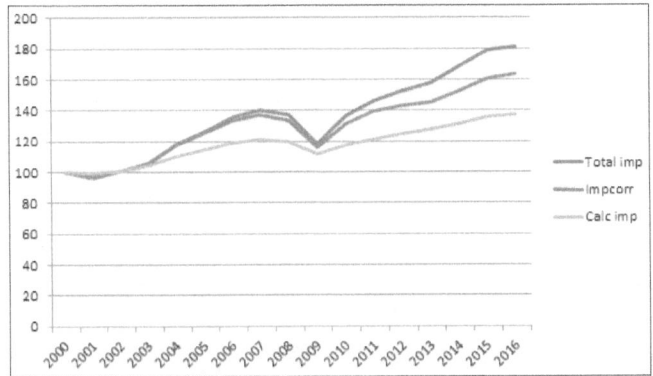

Source : data IMF, data US Census Bureau, Energy Intelligence Agency (EIA)

The ratio between domestic prices and import prices can be regarded as one of the variables to explain the market loss in domestic production.

Graph 3 Ratio Domestic Price And Import Price

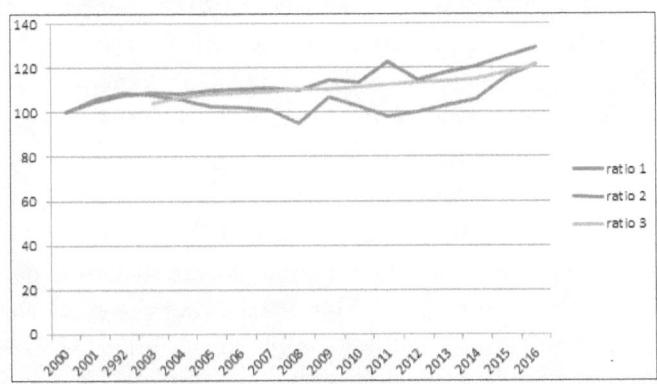

Source : IMF, US Census Bureau, EIA

As is illustrated in graph 3 prices of domestic production have increased a little more compared to import prices (ratio 1), especially in the second half of the reference period. When corrected for oil imports the difference becomes larger. The price ratio between domestic prices and the corrected import price (ratio 2) is more or less a steady upward trend. The same is true for the average price ratio of the last three years (ratio 3). Due to the fact that imported goods and services have become relatively cheaper, it is probable that some substitution of domestic production by imports has taken place. Using regression analysis it becomes clear that the calculated imports from the CPS matrix is the most dominant variable to explain the variance of the import volume. In a log linear specification the volume of imports (excluding oil) is explained by the calculated imports from the CPS matrix and the (lagged) ratio of the domestic price and the import price (ratio 3). Fixing the coefficient of the calculated imports at 1^4, the elasticity of the price ratio reaches a value of 1,9.

$$LIMVN=1 \ LIMC +1,9*LCOMPV-0,906$$

$$(-) \qquad (9,13) \qquad (-8,97)^5$$

$$R^2=0,97$$

$$DW=1,490$$

Where IMVN=import volume excluding oil, IMC= the calculated import volume on the basis of final demand. COMPV=lagged competition term.[6] The estimated equation shows a considerable impact of the competition term. An increase of the competition term of 1 % causes an increase of the import- volume by 1,9 %. The values between brackets correspond to the t statistics.

These values are a measure to test if a coefficient is zero (that is if the variable does not belong in the regression). If the t-statistic exceeds two in magnitude it is at least 95 % likely that the coefficient is not zero. In the equation the t value is 9,13 which means that the coefficient of the lagged competition term is not zero with a probability of 95 %. The t value of the calculated imports cannot be measured because the coefficient

---

[4] This means that if the competition term does not change the volume of imports will grow at the same rate as the volume of the calculated imports on the basis of final demand.

[5] The figures between brackets are t values, which give an indication whether the coefficient is significant, in general a value above 2,0 must be achieved.

[6] LIMVN=Ln (IMVN), LCOMPV=Ln(COMPV). COMPV=competition term last three years.

is fixed at a value of 1. The R^2 indicates that 97 % of the variation of LIMVN is explained by the regression line. The value of the Durbin Watson statistic is about 1,5, often a danger sign for autocorrelation. In the case of autocorrelation the residuals are not independent but correlated from different observations. The impact of (positive) autocorrelation is underestimating the standard error of the coefficients and an inflated t ratio. This means that it is possible that coefficients will be found to be significantly different from zero when in fact they are not. There are two kinds of models to circumvent this problem [7]: an autoregressive model and a moving average model. In an autoregressive model the dependent variable is explained not only by the explanatory variables, but also by previous variables of the dependent variable. In a moving average model the output variable depends linearly on current and past values of the error terms. In the case of the import equation a moving average model of the first order proved to give the best results. This means that in the estimation procedure the current error term and the error term of the year before are taken into account.[8] The transformed import relation shows the same coefficient for the competition term (1,9), whereas the t ratio remains about the same as well as the R^2. The Durbin Watson variable increases to 1,84, making it possible to accept the hypothesis of no autocorrelation.

2B Exports

In 2016 the US exported for 2216 billion dollars, of which 66 % goods and 34 % services. [9]During the reference period the share of services in exports has increased rapidly. In 2000 this share was only 27 %. So exports have become more service oriented. The composition of the exported goods is illustrated in table 3.

---

[7] Another solution, which will not be discussed is the introduction of a new explanatory variable in the import-equation.

[8] For more information look at extensive literature on this subject, e.g. Box, George; Jenkins, Gwilym. M. ; Reinsel Gregory C (1994) Time series Analysis: Forecasting and Control (Third Edition), Prentice Hall

[9] US Census Bureau

Table 3: Composition of exported goods (%) in 2016

Foods Etc	9,0
Crude Oil And Oil Products	6,1
Industrial Supplies	21,2
Capital Goods	35,8
Automotive Vehicles	10,4
Consumer Goods	13,4
Other Goods	4,1
Total	1,00

Source : US Census Bureau

The most important export categories are capital goods, industrial supplies (including crude oil and oil products) and consumer goods. The main importers of US goods are the European Union, Canada, Mexico, China and Japan. Exports are triggered by global demand, represented by the volume of world trade with an assumed elasticity of 1. Another factor is the competition with other countries. Graph 4 shows the development of world trade and the export volume of the US with and without a correction for the exports of crude and oil products.

Graph 4: Export Volume US, Export Volume US Corrected For Oil, World Trade during 2000-2016 (index 2000=100).

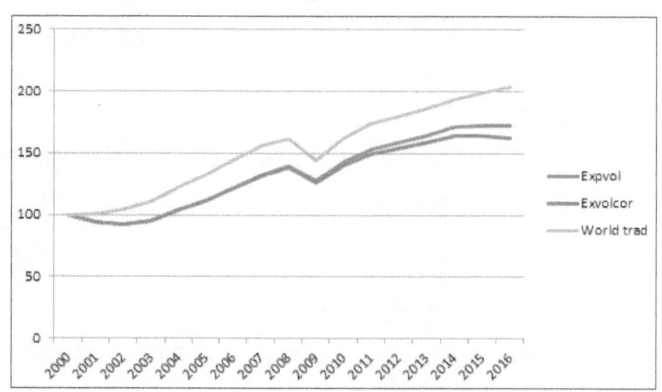

Source US Census Bureau, EIA, IMF database

Export volume growth lags behind the volume growth of world trade, but has the same conjunctural pattern. Whereas world trade volume grew by 4,6 % per annum during 2000-2016, export volume increased with 3,4 % in the same period. For exports excluding crude oil and oil products the volume growth was even smaller (3,1 % per annum). This means that some market loss on the international markets had to be accepted. China, but also Japan and Germany had a considerable surplus on their trade balance of the top 30 export industries.

Graph 5: World trade volume, export volume Japan, Germany, US 2000-2016 (index 2000=100)

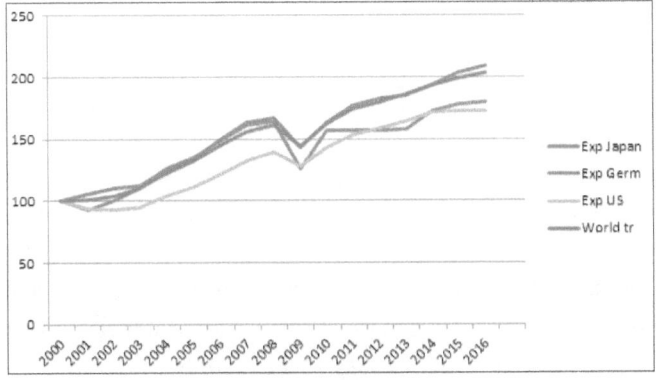

Source IMF database

The export volume of Germany follows the development of world trade or increases a little more in some years. The growth in export volume of Japan is more or less in line with the volume growth of world trade during the first half of the reference period, but in the second half Japan lagged behind. Never the-less Japan achieved somewhat better than the US. Export champion was China with an average increase of export volume of 14,2 % during 2000-2016,more than three times higher than world trade growth. Let us see whether price differences can explain the market loss of the US export sector. It is difficult to find a representative price indicator for the competing export. The export price for manufactured goods in advanced economies is presented here. Graph 5 describes the development of the price of exports (excl. oil) and the international export price of manufactures during 2000-2016. In addition the ratio between the export price (corrected for oil) and the export price of manufactures is illustrated.

Graph 6: Export Price US (Corrected For Oil) And Competing World Trade Price (Index 2000=100)

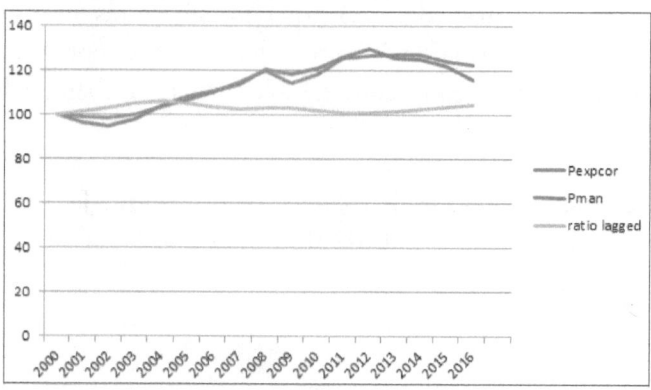

Source : IMF database, EIA

Export prices of US follow in general the development of the export price of manufactures in advanced economies, but in 2000-2003 and 2014-2016 the index of world prices was lower than the export price index of the US. If we introduce a lagged price ratio, which consists of the average ratio of the export price (excl. crude) and the price of manufactures of the last three years, then this ratio is higher than 2000 for the whole period. Using this variable in the estimation the price elasticity appears to be significant with a value of -2,5 (see also the estimated export equation below). Besides cost differences, currency policies and dumping practices can also play a role with regard to price differences. However it is likely that more factors have influenced the export performance of the US. Therefore it is necessary to look at supply factors. An important supply factor is the capacity to produce modern products and to enter new foreign markets. An indicator for this capacity is the relative investment ratio. This variable can be defined as the ratio between the Investment/GDP of the US and the weighted Investment/GDP ratio of the main competing countries. The higher this ratio, the better the competitiveness of the US economy.

Graph 7: The relative investment ratio of the US during 2000-2016.

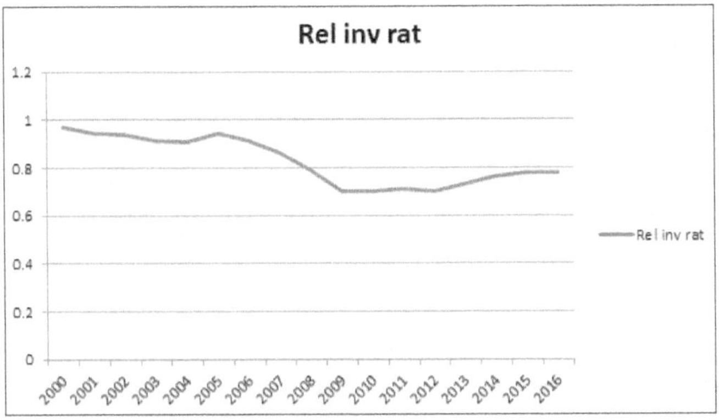

Source IMF database

The relative investment ratio of the US declined by 20 % during 2000-2016, caused by a slight increase of the average investment/GDP ratio of competitors and a declining ratio in the US. The slight increase in the average investment/GDP ratio of competitors is determined by the increase of this ratio in China, Canada and India, which overcompensate the modest decline in other countries. The decline of the relative investment ratio of the US could have harmed the competitiveness of the US economy and could have contributed to a part of the market loss on the export market. In the equation below the coefficient of the average relative investment rate of the past three years proved to be significant with a value of 0,28[10]. If this value is true, then the relative investment ratio together with the lagged price ratio can explain the reduced share of the US in world trade.

The following (log linear) equation was estimated[11]:

$$\text{Lexvn= 1 Lwhn -2,45Lpcom2v+0,28Lriyv+11,27}^{12}$$

$$(-) \qquad (-5,5) \qquad (4,6) \qquad (5,5)^{13}$$

---

[10] This value corresponds with the value found in the export relation for the Netherlands in a study of 1992: FKSEC a macro econometric model for the Netherlands (Central Planning Bureau).

[11] The coefficient of the volume of world trade was fixed at a value of 1.

[12] Lexvn=Ln(Exvn), L(pcomp2v)=Lnpcomp2v, Lriyv=Ln(riyv)

[13] The figures between brackets are t-values, which give an indication whether the coefficient is significant.

R^2= 0,985

DW=0,906

Where :whn= the volume of world trade, pcom2v= lagged competition term, riyv=the relative investment ratio of the US of the last three years. The R^2 gives an indication for the goodness of fit and is satisfactory, whereas the coefficients of all the explanatory variables are significant, except for the coefficient of world trade, which has been fixed at the value of 1. However the value of the Durbin Watson variable is too low, what makes it impossible to accept the hypothesis that there is no autocorrelation. Therefore a moving average model of the first order was used to avoid possible autocorrelation. The coefficients of the lagged competition term and the relative investment ratio do not change, whereas the t values increase to 8,4 for the competition term and 6,9 for the relative investment ratio. So these coefficients remain highly significant. The Durbin Watson value increases to 1,86 and makes it possible to accept the hypothesis of no autocorrelation. The R^2 improves a little. Institutions, such as the degree of openness of the international trading system, have an impact on international trade and thus on US exports, whereas the market position of US exporters influences the price elasticity. The lower the price elasticity the stronger the market position of US exporters. According to the estimated equation the market loss on the international market during 2000-2016 can for 30 % be ascribed to the decline of the relative investment rate and for 70 % as a result of relative prices. Due to the high elasticity of relative prices, there is some contribution of the competition term in spite of the modest development of the (lagged) price term. The consequences of the export performance and imports for the trade balance will be briefly discussed below.

2C Trade Balance

On the trade balance the values of imports and exports are registered. The volume and prices of imports and exports are already discussed above. Graph 5 illustrates the development of the exports and imports in current prices during 2000-2016.

Graph 8 Exports And Imports In Current Prices During 2000-2016

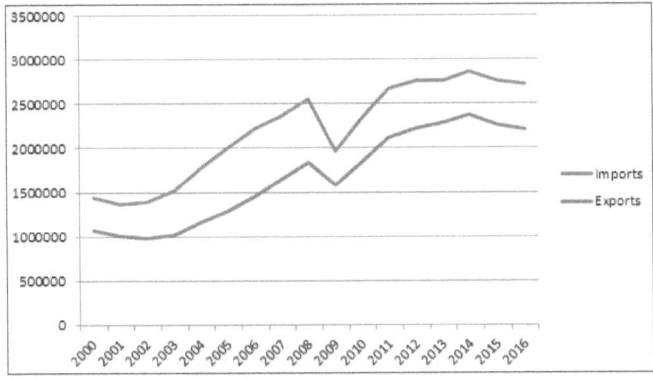

Source US Census Bureau

During the entire reference period there was a deficit on the trade balance. However in terms of GDP the deficit fluctuated from 3,6 % in 2000 to 5,5 % in 2006 and then declined to 2,7 % in 2016. The decrease of the deficit in the last part of the period was due to the increase in domestic oil production, causing less imports and more exports. Nevertheless the gap between imports and exports represents no less than 23 % of total exports in 2016. This means that even if total imports would remain constant, exports would have to grow by 23 % to close the gap.

3 Impact of Market Loss on GDP

To calculate the impact of market loss on GDP a few questions must be answered:

- What would have been the volume of imports if market share would have maintained on the level of 2000?
- What would have been the volume of exports if exports would have followed the volume of world trade?
- What would have been the consequences for the growth in GDP?

In table 2 is indicated that during 2000-2016 the volume of imports has increased by 3,1 % per annum or 64 % from 2000. In case of constant market share the volume of imports would have risen by 2 % per annum or 37,2 %. This means a reduction of imports of 0,390 trillion USD in prices of 2000 or 27 % in terms of imports in 2000.

Table 4 Export Volume 2000 And 2016 And
Export Volume Without Market Loss

(index 2000=100)

	2000	2016
Export Volume	100	172,4
Export Volume Without Market Loss	100	203,8
Market Loss (% Exports In 2000)		32

Table 4 indicates that if export volume would have followed world trade volume, exports would have had an additional increase of 32 % from 2000 or 0,340 trillion USD in prices of 2000. A reduction of imports and a rise of exports would have had a positive impact on the balance of payment and GDP. The impact of a constant market share on GDP can be calculated by the formula of GDP : $Y = CP + GO + INV + X - M$, where Y= GDP, CP=private consumption, GO=government consumption, INV=total investments, X= exports, M=imports. This means that : $\Delta Y = \Delta CP + \Delta GO + \Delta INV + \Delta X - \Delta M$. The primary impact of a constant market share on the domestic and foreign markets on GDP : $\Delta Y_o = \Delta X_o - \Delta M_o$, where ΔX= the primary impact on exports in prices of 2000 and ΔM= the primary impact on imports in prices of 2000. In terms of GDP of 2000 this would mean a rise of 3,3 % due to a better export performance and 3,8 % increase as a result of reduced imports.[14] All in all an increase of 7,1 %. However this is only the first impact on GDP. The additional GDP will cause a rise in domestic final demand (CP+GO+INV) and M to meet final demand. After the first period there will be an additional increase of GDP: $\Delta Y_1 = \alpha \Delta Y_o - m\alpha \Delta Y_o = \alpha(1-m)\Delta Y_o$, where α is the marginal propensity to spend and m=the marginal import rate. After the second period the impact on additional GDP will be:

$$\Delta Y_2 = \alpha\alpha(1-m)\Delta Y_o - m\alpha\alpha(1-m)\Delta Y_o = \alpha(1-m)\alpha(1-m)\Delta Y_o = (\alpha(1-m))^2 \Delta Y_o$$

After period n the influence on additional GDP will be : $\Delta Y_n = (\alpha(1-m))^n \Delta Y_o$ If $n \to \infty$ then the total impact will be : $(1/(1-\alpha(1-m))\Delta Y_o$. The multiplier in the equation is $1/(1-\alpha(1-m))$. The higher α the higher the multiplier, the higher m the lower the impact on GDP, as there is a higher leakage of income to foreign countries. If we limit ourselves to the effect of additional GDP on private consumption[15], the α equals the marginal propensity to consume and $m\alpha$ then is the marginal import rate due to private consumption. With a value of 0,85 for α and a value of 0,20 for m in 2000[16], the multiplier in the US is 3,1. This means that in the long run the impact on GDP of a constant market share on the domestic and foreign

[14] Taking into account the value of GDP in 2000 of 10,285 trillion dollars.

[15] Private consumption is by far the most important final demand category in the US.

[16] Rates for the period 2000-2016, measured in constant prices.

market can be estimated at 22 %. However this result must be handled with care due to the stylized approach and some implicit assumptions. A more sophisticated method would be to use a macroeconomic model, which can calculate the impact on final demand and the dynamics in the economy better. Furthermore it is assumed that the exchange rate remains stable in spite of the improvement in the balance of payment. Another assumption is that foreign competitors do not react. Due to the uncertainties of the long term approach we will only use the primary impact of the balance of payment improvement on GDP by sector.

3A Impact on GDP by sector

Production by sector has shown quite some differences during 2000-2016. Industry, Wholesale etc, Public Administration and Other Services show a lower than average production growth. Production in the construction sector even declined. The Agricultural sector, Information and Communication, Real estate, Professional services achieved a more than average increase.

Table 5: Average Growth GDP (%) By Sector
2000-2016, Shares By Sector In 2016

Agr	I	Con	W	Inf	Fin	Real	Prof	Publ Adm	Other serv	Total
2,9	1,4	-1,1	1,3	5,2	1,8	2,4	2,0	1,5	0,2	1,8
0,01	0,15	0,04	0,16	0,06	0,08	0,13	0,12	0,22	0,03	1,00

Source : Value added by activity, OECD data

Where Agr = agricultural sector, I=industry incl. energy, W=wholesale sector, Inf= information and communication, Fin = financial sector and insurance, Real= real estate, Prof= professional and scientific services, Publ. adm.= public administration, Other serv. = other services

The market loss on the domestic and foreign markets had a negative impact on the activities by sector. However this impact is not easy to calculate due to the lack of a sector model. However it is fair to assume that sectors with a relatively high exposure to foreign competition with regard to their exports as well as on the domestic market due to the competing imports will in general have suffered more than other sectors. There are clearly two groups of branches : the exposed and the sheltered activities. In the exposed sectors such as the manufacturing industry and the agricultural sector the market loss could have been substantial with a significant effect on employment. This means in the case of the manufacturing industry the loss of well paid jobs. In other sectors the impact would have been less e.g. in the construction sector, real estate[17] or wholesale sector.[18]

---

[17] However we have not taken into account the impact of higher economic growth on investments, so the impact on the construction and real estate sector. will probably be underestimated.

[18] For the public sector the impact is low. However we do not take into account the influence of more tax income as a result of higher economic growth

4 LABOR MARKET

Demand for labor was highly influenced by the economic developments. From 2000-2007 employment rose, but as a result of the crisis dropped till 2012,when a recovery took place. During the whole reference period GDP grew by 1,8 % per annum, while labor productivity increased with 1,2 % per year. This caused a rise in total employment with 0,6 % per annum. There were substantial differences in the development of employment by sector. In the agricultural sector employment remained stable but in the sector industry, mining, utilities and construction a decline occurred, whereas in the service sector (including government) a rise could be registered. The reduction of market share on the domestic and international market has depressed demand for labor especially in the manufacturing industry. In this sector the number of employees decreased from 19,644 million persons in 2000 to 15,408 million in 2016[19]. If there would not have been a market loss, production would have been considerably higher and the loss of employment would have been considerably lower. [20]

In the past a lot of low skilled jobs have disappeared as a result of technological developments in combination with competition by low wage countries. Supply of labor increased by 0,7 % per annum. The supply of labor is defined as the sum of employment and unemployed people. Unemployed people are people who are without work, are available for the labor market and actively seeking work. Unemployment amounted to 4 % of the total labor force in 2000, but during the period 2008-2010 a level of 9,6 % was reached. After 2010 unemployment declined to 4,9 % in

---

[19] Definition OECD.

[20] calculations with input output analysis.

2016. However this figure conceals some problems on the labor market. The participation rate for the population of 16 years and over has declined from 67,1 % in 2000 to 62,8 % in 2016. There are several reasons for this drop. In the first place increased schooling caused people to postpone their participation of the labor market. Then there is the aging of the population, which has resulted in a growing number of people who leave the labor force due to retirement. Poor health and / or disability has been a reason for a growing number of people to be out of the labor market. A growing number of (jobless) persons are not actively looking for a job, so they are not registered as unemployed. Due to the lack of skills some people find it hard to get a job and leave the workforce. Other people can only obtain low paid service jobs which are unattractive for some of them.

Table 6: Labor force shares, employment shares and unemployment rates by age and sex in 2002 and 2016

	Labor force shares (%)		Employment shares (%)		Unemployment rates (%)	
Groups	2002	2016	2002	2016	2002	2016
Young	15,4	13,3	14,4	12,5	13,6	10,4
Prime	70,2	64,2	71,0	64,8	5,1	4,2
Older	14,4	22,5	14,6	22,7	4,0	3,6
Sex						
Men	53,4	53,2	53,4	53,2	5,9	4,9
Women	46,6	46,8	46,6	46,8	5,6	4,8

Young=16-24 years, Prime=25-54 years, Older=55 years and over
Source : Bureau of Labor Statistics

Table 7 Labor force shares, employment shares and unemployment rates by skill of population (25 years and older) in 2002 and 2016

Level	Labor force shares (%)		Employment shares (%)		Unemployment rates (%)	
	2002	2016	2002	2016	2002	2016
1	10,3	7,7	9,9	7,5	8,4	7,4
2	30,9	25,8	30,6	25,5	5,3	5,2
3	27,4	27,5	27,5	27,5	4,5	4,1
4	31,4	39,0	32,0	39,5	2,9	2,5

Level 1=Less than High School, level 2=High School Graduates, level 3= Some College and Associate Degree, level 4= Bachelor's Degree and higher
Source : Bureau of Labor Statistics

Table 6 shows the ageing of the labor force and employment as the share of older employees increases during 2002-2016 at the cost of that of young people and especially prime aged persons. Unemployment rates have declined somewhat in 2016 compared to 2002[21], but in both years the unemployment rate of young people is much higher than those of the other groups. Labor force and employment shares by sex have remained stable during the period mentioned above. From table 7 it becomes clear that the composition of the labor force (25 years and older) and employment have shifted from level 1 and level 2 to level 4, from lower skills to high skills. Unemployment rates decreased a little for all levels, but the unemployment rate of level 4 is lower than those of other skill levels, especially those of level 1 and 2. Table 7 does not give an indication about the quality of education and the composition of the educational system by subject. These factors will be discussed later. Wage development during 2000-2016 has been tempered by the slow increase of labor demand. Real average wages did only partly follow the trend of labor productivity. This was most pronounced in the lower and middle ranges of the earnings scale

---

[21] Compared to 2000 the unemployment rate increased in 2016.

Globalization and immigration have increased competition at these skill levels. Therefore a significant increase in earnings inequality has occurred.

As a result the share of labor compensation in total GDP (current national prices) decreased from 0,64% in 2000 to 0,59 % in 2016.[22] Without the described loss of market share more jobs could have been saved in the manufacturing industry, which would have had a positive impact on wages.

---

[22] Figures Federal Reserve

5 GOVERNMENT BUDGET

Government revenues amounted to 5731627 million dollar or 31 % of GDP in 2016. The most important category consists of income taxes, followed by social security contributions. Other categories are ad valorem taxes, fees and charges and business revenues. Compared to other OECD countries the tax structure of the United states is characterized by :

- Substantial higher revenues from taxes on personal income, profits and gains and higher revenues from taxes on property and goods and services.
- A lower proportion of revenues from taxes on corporate income and gains and social security contributions
- No revenues from taxes on payroll and value added taxes Income tax can be divided in direct taxes on wage income, transfer income and non wage income.

In determining taxes from wage income and transfer income we distinguish a quantity component (number of wage earners etc) and a price component (wage rate or level of benefits). Direct taxes on non wage income are calculated as the sum of direct taxes on imputed income of self employed and direct taxes on other non wage income of households (consisting of interest payments, dividends etc).

Corporate taxes are determined as the tax tariff multiplied by the tax base. Ad valorem taxes are based on the value of goods and services. Government expenses were 6541465 million dollar in 2016 or 35 % of GDP. Government expenditure was dominated by government pensions, health care followed by government education, national defense and all other spending. Other spending includes wages and salaries, interest payments etc. Most categories can be divided in a quantity and price component. Some are influenced by macro economic factors (number of unemployed in the case of unemployment benefits, wages by inflation, interest rate in the case of interest payments). Others are determined by political preferences.

If the US had been able to maintain its market share on domestic and foreign markets the economic growth and employment would have been larger. Wages would have been higher too, taking into account the improved situation on the labor market. There would also have been a higher inflation. This would have created higher revenues from income taxes for the government as a result of higher employment, higher wages and more income from ad valorem taxes. On the other hand some additional expenses could be expected due to higher wages for government employees, higher expenses for purchasing goods and services, government expenses. However on balance the government deficit would have been lower than 4 % of GDP in 2016, provided that no additional non mandatory expenses would occur as a result of the improved budgetary situation. Owing to smaller deficits during the reference period government debt would have been lower and also interest payments would have dropped, causing a further improvement of the budgetary situation.

6 CONCLUSIONS REGARDING MARKET LOSS

Market loss on the domestic and international market has caused a decrease of economic growth, especially with regard to the manufacturing industry. It had a negative influence on the balance of payment, employment, government revenues and thus also on consumption and investments. The main question is how to improve the trade balance, reduce the government deficit, increase jobs in high value added sectors. To achieve better results an improvement of economic performance is necessary.

7 IMPROVEMENT ECONOMIC PERFORMANCE

Improvement of economic performance can be achieved by the following measures:[23]

7A Investing in skills

According to the OECD's new survey of Adult Skills of 2017 [24]the US score slightly above the OECD average with regard to proficiency in literacy. Countries like Japan, Finland, the Netherlands, Sweden and Norway have better scores. The situation regarding the proficiency in numeracy is worse as the US rank only 28 on the list of 34 countries and below the OECD average. In the case of problem solving in information-rich environments the US have a score which equals the OECD average. [25] Literacy skills stand for the ability to understand and respond appropriately to written texts, whereas numeracy deals with the ability to use numerical and mathematical concepts. Problem solving in information-rich environments is the capacity to access, interpret and analyze information found, transformed and communicated in digital environments.

---

[23] In chapter 8 more concrete policies will be mentioned, especially regarding the innovation system.

[24] PIAAC : Survey of Adult Skills, 2017

[25] All scores are derived from the PIAAC survey comparing scores from 2013-2016 for proficiency in literacy, numeracy and problem solving.

An upgrading of skills will be an on-going necessity for all economies as changing skill requirements are accelerated by changing patterns of production, trade international competition and technological innovation. Action is needed to improve the basic skills of adults and to encourage their return to postsecondary education and training. One in four higher education graduates in the US has numeracy skills below level 2 on a scale that goes to level 5.There are large skill discrepancies between advantaged and disadvantaged 15-year old students. Having poor skills represents a major barrier to finding a productive and rewarding job and is also associated with low hourly wages when employed. As the returns to skills in the US are among the largest in OECD countries it can be expected that better skills can also lead to less wage inequality. Better skills can also prevent a mismatch on the labor market. The US is strongly specialized in technology advanced industries, particularly more complex business services and high tech manufacturing. However according to the OECD this specialization pattern does not fully match the countries skills characteristics. This can make it hard to maintain this specialization in view of the increasing competition and to introduce new similar industries.

7B Promote a level playing field with regard to foreign trade partners[26]

The US have always encouraged free trade and signed many trade agreements, which were meant to remove trade barriers. These agreements were based on classic free trade theory, which holds that free trade benefits all countries by allowing each to specialize in producing the product or services for which they have a comparative advantage. According to this theory international economic welfare would be maximized, consumers would have access to products with the highest value, lowest cost products and services. This is true as long as everybody plays by the rules. However many countries are cheating in order to win the competition race. This is caused by manipulation of currencies, markets, intellectual property rights, standards, foreign technology and direct investments. The goal is not to

---

[26] See also Innovation Economics by Robert D. Atkinson and Stephen J. Ezell,2012

increase the global supply of jobs or productivity or innovation, but a shift in production to the cheating countries.

Especially China has been manipulating its currency in order to maintain a strong competitive position. The renminbi has been kept low in the past. In this way Chinese exports were subsidized and imports had become artificially more expensive. This caused large surpluses on the balance of payment which were not spend. As a result massive current account reserves emerged. Such a policy undermines the trust in the positive effects of free trade. Another drawback is that it artificially shifts world production to more labor and away from capital, because labor is artificially subsidized. Other measures to promote exports by the Chinese government are direct subsidies to steel and other products, which lower the export price. As a condition of operating in the country China forces multinational companies in technology-based industries to share technologies with Chinese state owned companies in a joint venture. In this way the Chinese get the technology for free in exchange for business opportunities.

Another instrument to curb imports is the existence of discriminatory product standards. These standards are meant to keep out foreign products. Import duties for some products were introduced to protect domestic production. Monopolies exist on the domestic Chinese market. They are an obstacle for US companies to compete. The above mentioned mercantilist practices have enabled citizens in the US to buy artificially cheap products from China, but at the cost of production and employment losses in the US. For China these practices have caused additional production and employment, but the impact on welfare has been dampened by the unfavorable terms of trade, the export subsidies and import duties.

It remains to be seen whether the intellectual property theft will benefit developing countries in the long run. In the long run there will presumably insufficient incentives to develop and adopt homegrown technology developments.

In order to achieve a level playing field the US should detect Chinese policies, which violates the rules or the spirit of the World Trade Organization. However this should be done without creating a trade war. Since 2001 China has been a member of the WTO. However this organization has failed to act sufficiently against the mercantilist policies of China.[27] The impact of trade with China on the balance of payment of the US is substantial. In 2018 the trade deficit with China amounted to 379 billion dollars[28], 61 % of the total trade deficit of the US. In 2000 the trade gap with China was only 82 billion dollars. These facts underline the necessity of the following measures:

- Establish an Industrial Intelligence Unit within the National Intelligence Council. This Unit should gather information concerning foreign innovation, mercantilism. The National Intelligence Council could also be involved in developing and coordinating a response to damaging trade practices from foreign countries.

The United States Trade Representative's Office could identify violations of WTO regulations and hurtful foreign policies and practices that do not necessarily violate the WTO. More transparency should be obtained to detect what Chinese entities are interested in Foreign Direct Investments in the US. In general new rules, transparency procedures and enforcement mechanisms could be introduced as an ultimate alternative of the WTO. These measures could ensure an open, transparent and enforceable rules- and market-based trade and economic system. In order to influence negotiations about a level playing field with China president Trump has introduced taxes on Chinese exports to the US and announced further taxation in the near future. So far a tax of 10 % on Chinese exports of 200 billion dollars is realized and a further taxation of 25 % on an export value of 50 billion dollars. On May 10th 2019 Trump has increased import tariffs on $200 billion of imported Chinese products to 25 %. This tariff will increase to 30 % on October 1.

Furthermore on September 1 2019 Trump has imposed a 10 % tax on an additional 300 billion dollars of China's exports to the US. It is not easy to calculate the impact of these measures if they are fully carried out. Taxes on imports mean higher import prices and higher prices of domestic production and consumption. Higher prices of imports will affect

---

[27] In order to force change at the World Trade Organization, the US blocked the appointment of judges of the WTO Appellate Body, which acts as a supreme court for inter national trade.

[28] Office of US trade representative. Figures comprise goods and services.

the competitiveness of imported Chinese goods and imports of Chinese goods will decrease. The impact could be substantial. So the US industry could benefit from the taxation if a substitution to domestic production is feasible.[29] If the higher taxes will be passed through to the domestic market consumer prices will increase and in turn will influence wages in the future. Producers will face a modest impact on their input prices and could raise their prices a little.

The impact on GDP is difficult to calculate. Higher consumer prices will decrease the purchasing power of the consumer and have a negative effect on GDP, whereas a possible substitution of Chinese goods by domestic production will have a positive influence on GDP and employment. A trade war can cause a disruption of the supply chain with a negative impact on domestic production. On the other hand a successful substitution of Chinese products by products of other foreign (Asian) countries can decrease possible supply problems.

Another factor which has not been taken into account is the exchange rate. The Chinese Renminbi could devaluate and decrease the price increases as a result of the taxation and the impact on Chinese imports. In August 2019 the Renmimbi has sunk to 7 against the dollar, the lowest value in 11 years. The US has accused China of currency manipulation. Furthermore there is the retaliation from China. This country has introduced taxation on imported US products and thus damage US exports. However China is not able to react symmetrically to US duties due to the trade gap. So far China has set tariffs on 185 billion dollars. But it can make life uneasy for US companies to operate in China.

All in all the policy of taxation could force China to make concessions, but the risk of a trade war cannot be underestimated. On this moment negotiations of the US with China are still going on.[30] Whatever the outcome may be, there will be a continuous China-US geopolitical competition, which sometimes takes the form of a technology battle. The best way to win this battle is to introduce a robust innovation system, which

---

[29] But this substitution probably comes with higher prices, as production costs in the US are generally higher than in China.

[30] In December 2019 there a provision agreement was signed postponing new taxation on Chinese goods and reducing the existing taxation. In exchange China will import additional agricultural goods from the US with a value of 25 billion dollars.

will be described below. Another solution is to develop a trade system which creates a level playing field with foreign competitors.

Recently the US has reached an agreement with Canada and Mexico in the framework of a renewal of the North American Trade Agreement (NAFTA). According to the Administration the agreement will create a more balanced, reciprocal trade that supports high-paying jobs for Americans and boosts the North American Economy.

Important features of the agreement are:

- The creation of a more level playing field for American workers, including improved rules of origin for automobiles, trucks, other products and disciplines on currency manipulations.
- Benefiting American farmers, ranchers and agribusinesses by modernizing and strengthening food and agricultural trade in North America.
- Supporting a 21st Century economy through new protection for US intellectual property and ensuring opportunities for trade in US services.
- New chapters covering Digital Trade, Anticorruption and Good Regulatory Practices as well as a chapter devoted to ensuring that small and Medium Sized

Enterprises benefit from the Agreement. The new United States-Mexico-Canada Agreement must be finalized and implemented.

7C Winning the race by a robust innovation system

Innovation is the driving force for productivity growth, which in turn is the main factor for potential output growth. Potential output is the production which belongs to the structural labor supply, corrected for the equilibrium unemployment [31] and the level of structural labor productivity.

---

[31] The equilibrium unemployment is defined as the level of employment that results after correction for incidental and conjunctural factors and is at the same time the level of employment that results after adjustment processes have taken place. (see : F.J.H. Don, the medium term Dutch growth potential, 2001)

Table 8: Labor productivity growth in the US and
other countries 1990-2016 (% per annum)

	1990/2000	1995/2000	2000/2005	2005/2010	2010/2016
US	1,5	2,4	1,9	1,3	0,6
Adv econ	1,8	2,2	1,5	0,9	0,7
Germany	2,3	1,7	0,8	0,1	0,8
France	1,4	2,5	1,0	0,3	0,4
Japan	0,8	1,1	1,5	0,3	0,6
Canada	1,4	1,9	0,8	0,1	1,0
Korea	5,8	4,7	3,2	3,0	1,4

Source IMF

Table 9: GDP constant prices per capita (% per annum)[32]

	1990/1995	1995/2000	2000/2005	2005/2010	2010/2016
Mexico	0,1	3,9	0,2	0,2	1,8
China	12,3	7,6	9,1	10,7	7,1

Source IMF

Table 8 shows an acceleration of productivity growth in the US from 1995-2005. An important factor for this acceleration was the application of IT by businesses. After 2004 the impact of IT on additional productivity growth gradually disappeared. During 2005-2010 the great recession took place, but due to the flexibility of the US economy a collapse of labor productivity could be prevented. A lot of less productive employees were fired causing a modest increase of overall productivity. In the period 2010-2016 the economy recovered and the employees were hired again. This development had in turn a negative impact on labor productivity. Presumably this impact will only be temporary, so it is widely assumed that labor productivity increase will return to a higher value in the years to come. During 1990-2016 the US had a slightly higher productivity growth compared to the efficiency gains in the advanced economies as a whole and a higher productivity growth with regard to countries like Germany, Japan and France. Countries like Korea and China (in terms of GDP per

---

[32] As employment figures were not available for these countries GDP in constant prices per capita were presented

capita) showed a much bigger productivity increase than the US, although some of these efficiency gains may be used to catch up with the advanced economies.

In general economists do not expect economic growth in the US during the coming 10 years to return to levels of more than 3 % per annum like in the period 1990-2005. The reason is that the expected labor productivity growth will be modest (1-1,5 % per annum) without another burst of information technology induced productivity growth and that labor force will increase by only 0,5 % per annum due to demographic developments. However efficiency gains can be influenced by adequate measures to improve innovation. Improvement of the innovation system could improve the rate of growth of the of the US economy, its competitiveness, restore equilibrium on the balance of payment, and promote the creation of well paid jobs. In order to formulate strategies for improving the innovation system information from the Global Innovation Index (GII) can be used. This index describes the factors that influences innovation and provides a database for 127 countries, representing 92,5 % of the world's population and 97,6 % of global GDP. The GII is published by Cornell University, INSEAD and the world Intellectual Property Organization (WIPO, an agency of the United Nations). Data are obtained from more than 30 sources. Hard data are preferred over qualitative assessments. The GII is determined by two sub-indices - the Innovation Input

Sub-Index and the Innovation Output Sub-Index, each built around key pillars. Five input pillars comprise factors that enable innovation: (1) **institutions,** (2) **Human capital and research,** (3) **Infrastructure,** (4) **Market sophistication** and (5) **Business sophistication.** Two output pillars can be distinguished: (6) **Knowledge and technology outputs** and (7) **Creative outputs.** Each input pillar has a weight of 0, 10 in total GII, the weight of each output pillar in total GII is 0,25. Each pillar can be divided in sub-pillars and each sub-pillar is composed of individual indicators (81 in total in 2018)[33]. Sub-pillar scores (0-100) are calculated as the weighted average of individual indicators; pillar scores are determined as the weighted average of sub-pillar scores.

---

[33] Due to the high number of individual indicators these variables will only be briefly mentioned.

The following variables can be calculated:

- Innovation input Sub-index : the simple average of the first five pillar scores.
- Innovation Output Sub-index : the simple average of the last two pillar scores.
- The overall GII score : the simple average of the input and output Sub-index.
- The innovation Efficiency ratio : the ratio of the Output Sub-index over the input Sub-index.

With the help of the scores of the several indices we can compare and rank the innovation system of the US with the situation in other countries. In 2018 the US rank 6 with regard to the Global Innovation Index [34]. In spite of the high ranking of the US other countries can have better scores for their pillars and sub-pillars than the US.

In table 10 the scores of the pillars for the US and some other high ranking countries (Germany, Singapore, Switzerland, Sweden, Denmark en Hong Kong) are illustrated. Now we can compare the achievement by pillar of the US with the achievement of the country with the highest score of that pillar. For **institutions and human capital and research** Singapore has the highest score, for **Infrastructure** Hong Kong is the top country, for **market sophistication** the US are leading, for **business sophistication** the Netherlands together with Singapore are the top countries.

For **knowledge and technology output** as well as for **creative output** Switzerland is ahead of all other nations.

---

[34] In the following chapters the Global Innovation Index will be referred to as GII.

Table 10: Scores US and other countries by pillar for 2018

	US	Germ	Sing	Switz	Swe	Den	Hong	Neth	Diff US with top country
Institutions	87,7	85,9	94,7	88,9	89,6	91,1	89,4	90	7
Human Capital	51,3	58,7	73,3	64	62,2	63	47,5	56,5	22
Infra	58,8	60,5	65,8	65,3	67,1	62,3	68,9	62,4	10,1
Market soph	85,1	58,5	72,4	67,5	64,7	68,3	75,7	58,3	
Business soph	56,1	52,8	65,1	62,6	62,5	52,4	52	65,1	9
Knowl and tech output	55,6	52,2	51,3	74,9	60,1	46,9	36,7	63,7	19,3
Creative Output	48	53,3	39,6	59,4	53,8	51,7	48,4	56,7	11,4
Total Score	59,8	58,0	59,9	68,4	63,1	58,4	54,6	63,3	12,5

Germ=Germany, Sing=Singapore, Switz= Switzerland, Swe= Sweden, Den=Denmark, Hong=Hong Kong (China), Neth=Netherlands

Table 10 shows that in spite of the high score of the US with regard to *institutions,* Singapore and some other countries have a better achievement. **Institutions** comprise of the *political environment,* the *regulatory environment* and the *business environment.* According to the World Bank the US are the third country with regard to *business environment.* But the *political environment* and the *regulatory environment* could be improved[35]. The *political environment* is influenced by the political stability, absence of violence/terrorism and by government effectiveness. The political stability measures the perceptions of the likelihood of political instability and/or politically motivated violence including terrorism. Government effectiveness deals with perceptions of the quality of public services, the quality of civil service and the degree of its independence from political pressure, the quality of policy formulation and implementation and the credibility of the government's commitment to such policies. The *regulatory environment* can be divided into regulatory quality, the rule of law and

---

[35] See World Bank Governance Indicators, ease of doing business index

the cost of redundancy dismissal. The regulatory quality reflects the perceptions of the government to formulate and implement sound policies and regulations that permit and promote private sector development. The cost of redundancy dismissal is related to the flexibility of employment especially as it relates to the areas of hiring, working hours and redundancy.

The *business environment* is related to the ease of starting a business and the ease of resolving insolvency (see table 11). The US have a top score with regard to the *business environment*. However there is a difference in scores of 7 with Singapore for the pillar **institutions**, because that country has a better achievement regarding the *political and regulatory environment*.

The next pillar : **Human capital and research** can be divided into *education in general, tertiary education and research and development. Education in general* is related to expenditure on education, government expenditure on education per pupil (secondary) in terms of GDP per capita, school life expectancy, assessment in reading, mathematics and science, pupil teacher ratio (secondary).

For *education in general* in the US rank 47 out of 127 countries. Compared to some advanced countries (Switzerland, Korea, Germany, Singapore) the score of the US is somewhat lower, but the differences with countries like Finland, the Netherlands, Denmark, Sweden are bigger. The relatively high pupil- teacher ratio on secondary schools deserves attention (see table 11), whereas the US are not a top ten country with respect to the expenditure on education in % GDP, the government expenditure per pupil (secondary schools), school life expectancy (years) and the PISA scales in reading, mathematics and science.

In 2015 the pupil-teacher ratio on secondary schools amounted to 14,7 in the US, which is rather high compared to a lot of developed countries. Some people regard the average class size as a crude indicator of the quality of education. So legislative mandates on maximum class size have been very popular at the state level. However there are some objections against a further (general) decline of the class size. According to influential and credible studies class size reductions has been shown to work for some students in some grades and countries, but its impact has been found to be mixed and or not discernible in other settings and circumstances that seem similar. In this regard it is worth noting that the East Asian nations that perform at higher levels than the US on international exams have very large class sizes. Another objection of class size reduction is its high cost. Decreasing the pupil-teacher ratio in the US by one student would increase expenses by $12 billion dollars per year in teacher salary costs alone. So the costs and benefits of class-size mandates need to be carefully weighed against all of the alternatives.[36] Possible improvements of secondary (and primary) education will be discussed later on. The Programme for International Student Assessment (OECD)[37] develops triennial international surveys that examine 15 year old students performance in reading, mathematics and science. In this survey the US lag behind the other top 25 countries (see table 11). *Tertiary education* is related to tertiary enrolment (% of relevant population), graduates in science and engineering (% of all tertiary graduates) and tertiary- level inbound mobility. Tertiary-level inbound mobility is the number of students from abroad studying in a given country as a percentage of the total tertiary enrolment in that country. Attracting mobile students, especially if they stay permanently, is also a way to tap into a global pool of talent, compensate weaker educational capacity at lower educational levels, support the development of innovation and production systems and mitigate the impact of an ageing population on future skills supply.[38] With regard of *tertiary education* the US only rank 88 on the GII. This is the result of a low percentage of graduates in science and engineering and weak tertiary-level inbound mobility (see table 11).

Research and development is the last sub pillar of **human capital and research.** Indicators for this sub pillar are researchers in full time equivalent per million population, gross expenditure on research and development (% GDP), average expenditure on research and development of the top three global companies and the average score of the top three universities at the QS world university ranking. The US are the top country with regard of the average score of the top three universities and the average expenditure on research and development of the top three global companies (see table 11). Based on figures for 2014 the US spend 2,7 % of GDP on R&D expenses.[39] Some countries like Switzerland, Korea, Germany and Japan have a higher R&D figure than the US. That is why the US rank 10 in the

---

[36] See Class Size: What research says and what it means for state policy, report by M. Chingos and Grover Whitehurst, 2011

[37] Abbreviated PISA.

[38] see OECD quotations in ICEF monitor(a free market intelligence resource for the international education industry.

[39] Figure World Bank

---

world regarding R&D More than 70 % of the R&D expenses is invested by enterprises (situation 2017).

The US rank 4 in the field of *research and development* due to the excellent performance regarding the average expenditure on R&D by the top three global companies and the average score of the top three universities. However as a result of the poor performance regarding general education and tertiary education the US lag behind a lot of other countries as far as total **human capital and research** is concerned. The top country for this pillar is Singapore. This country scores 22 points more than the US.

The next pillar of the GII is **infrastructure**, which consists of *information and communication technologies (ICTs), general infrastructure and ecological sustainability. Information and communication technologies* have the following indicators:

ICT access, ICT use, government online service and online e-participation.

ICT access is related to the fixed telephone subscriptions per 100 inhabitants, mobile telephone subscriptions per 100 inhabitants, international internet bandwidth per internet user, percentage of households with a computer, percentage of households with internet.

ICT use depends on the percentage of individuals using the internet, fixed (wired) broadband internet subscriptions per 100 inhabitants and active mobile broadband subscriptions per 100 inhabitants. Government online service deals with the quality and possibilities of the national website in the native language, including the national portal, e-services portal and e-participation portal, as well as the websites of the related ministries of education, labor, social services, health, finance and environment.

Online e-participation is determined by the use of online services to facilitate provision of information by the government to citizens, interactions with stakeholders and engagement to decision making processes. Although the US do not belong to the top ten countries for most of the indicators of ICT, the difference with the scores of the top country (Singapore) is small.

The general infrastructure is determined by the electricity output (kwh per capita), logistic performance and gross capital formation (% of GDP). Logistics performance depends on the efficiency of customs and border management clearance, the quality of trade and transport infrastructure, the ease of competitively priced shipments, the competence and quality of logistics services-trucking, forwarding and customs brokerage, the ability of track and trace consignments and finally the frequency with which reach consignees within scheduled or expected delivery times. With reference to the electricity output per capita and the logistic performance the US belongs to the top ten countries in the world. The relatively low level of gross capital formation as a percentage of GDP is regarded as a weak point of the US economy (see table 11). The country ranks 92 among 127 countries.[40] In chapter 2 the market loss on foreign markets during 2000-2015 could partly be explained by the decreasing relative investment ratio of the US.

The *ecological sustainability* consists of the following indicators: The GDP per unit of energy use, the environmental performance and the number of ISO 14001 environmental certificates per billion GDP. ISO 14001 specifies the requirements for an environmental management system that an organization can use to enhance its environmental performance. The GDP per unit of energy use is an indication of the efficiency in energy use. A large GDP/unit of energy use means a high energy productivity and the other way around. The US have a relatively low energy productivity, which explains the low raking in this field (75). The environmental performance justifies a ranking of 26, whereas the ISO 14001 environmental certificates per billion GDP show a large negative difference of environmental management in the US compared to other industrialized countries. For the total pillar **infrastructure** the score of the US is 10,1 points lower than those of Hong Kong (the top country). The next pillar is **market sophistication. Market sophistication** depends on *the credit* market, *investment and trade, competition & market scale.* Indicators for the *credit market* are the ease of getting credit, domestic credit to the private sector (% GDP). The ease of getting credit refers to the strength of legal rights of lenders and borrowers, and to the depth of credit information. According to the GII the US are the top country in the world for the credit market.

The sub pillar *investment* is related to the ease of protecting minority investors, market capitalization (% GDP) and venture capital deals/billion of GDP (PPP)[41]. The ease of protecting minority investors depends on the extent of conflict of interest regulation and the extent of shareholder governance. The extent of conflict of interest regulation deals with the protection of shareholders against director's misuse of corporate assets for personal gain.

---

[40] Source IMF

[41] Purchasing Power Parity

The extent of shareholder governance depends among others on the shareholder's right and role in major corporate decisions, governance safeguards protecting shareholders from undue board control and entrenchment, transparency on ownership stakes, compensation, audits and financial prospects. A good protection of minority investors is favorable to attract new capital for investments and innovation. Market capitalization or market value is the share price times the number of shares outstanding for listed domestic companies, investment funds and unit trusts. A high market value indicates a healthy state of domestic companies, which makes it easy for them to invest in modern technology from internal sources or external sources. Venture capital deals are the number of deals per billion GDP(PPP).Venture capital is a type of private equity that is provided by firms or funds to small, early -stage, emerging funds, that is expected to have high growth potential. These start-ups are usually based on an innovative technology or business model and they are usually from the high technology industries, such as the information technology, clean technology or biotechnology. A relative high number of venture capital deals is an indication of an innovative economy. The US belong to the top five countries with regard to *investment. Trade, competition and market scale* can be divided into applied tariff rate, the intensity of local competition and the domestic market scale. A variable to measure the degree of openness of a country to trade with foreign countries is the weighted mean applied tariff rate of imported products. The US rank 50 with regard to the applied tariff rate (weighted mean in %).[42]

The intensity of local competition is derived by a survey. A strong local competition as in the US[43] can give incentives to innovation for enterprises in order to survive.

The domestic market scale is measured by GDP based on purchasing-power- parity (PPP) in current dollar prices. A large domestic market affects productivity by economies of scale in production and incentives for innovation. A large market size can enable productivity gains by specialization. Firms can also benefit from economies of scale in a large domestic market by producing more output with proportionally less input, caused by larger and more efficient capital equipment. Larger markets like

---

[42] Source: World Bank

[43] With a rank of 5

in the US[44] create substantially bigger incentives for generating new ideas. An important reason is that there are increasing returns to scale embedded in knowledge creation and technology.

According to the GII the US are the top country in the world with regard to **market sophistication**. This is based on a top raking with regard to *the credit* market, the *investment* situation and *trade, competition and market scale.* The large number of venture capital deals and the large domestic market are an indication of strength for the US economy.

The next pillar is **business sophistication.**

The US belong to the top ten countries with regard to **business sophistication**, although countries like Singapore (top country), Switzerland and Sweden have a somewhat higher score.

Business sophistication is linked to the situation around *knowledge workers, innovation linkages* and *knowledge absorption.* The situation around *knowledge workers* is determined by the knowledge intensive employment as a percentage of total employment, Gross Expenditure on R&D (GERD) performed by businesses (%GDP) and GERD financed by businesses (% total GERD). Whereas the US belong to the top ten countries in the world regarding GERD investment and GERD financing, employment in knowledge intensive services (% workforce) lags behind other developed countries like Singapore, Switzerland and Sweden. [45]

Innovation linkages are influenced by university/industry research collaboration, the state of cluster development, GERD financed by abroad, joint venture /strategic alliance deals per billion GDP (PPP), the number of patent families filed by residents in at least two different countries per billion GDP (PPP). According to a survey for the GII there is a close collaboration in the US between the universities and the industry, which is favorable for innovation.[46]

The US are a leading country in this respect and are the top country with regard to cluster development. Clusters are geographic concentrations of firms, suppliers producers of related products and services and specialized institutions in a particular field. Widespread and well developed, deep clusters are beneficial to knowledge production and innovation.

---

[44] Second best country

[45] The US rank 29 with respect to knowledge intensive employment (%)

[46] Source :World Economic Forum

GERD financed by abroad (%) is rather small, which puts the US on place 62.[47] The joint venture/ strategic deals per billion GDP in the US are not enough to achieve a top ten position in the world. This is also the case with respect to the number of patent families per billion GDP. A patent family is a set of interrelated applications filed in one or more countries or jurisdictions to protect the same invention. The patent system is designed to encourage innovation by providing innovators wit time-limited exclusive legal rights, thus enabling them to appropriate the returns from their innovative activity.

The third sub pillar of **business sophistication** is *knowledge absorption. Knowledge absorption* is related to intellectual property payments (% total trade), high-tech imports less re-imports (% total trade), ICT services imports (% total trade), Foreign Direct Investments (FDI) net inflows (% of GDP) and research talent in business enterprise (% total employment). Intellectual property payments stand for charges for the use of intellectual property (% total trade). Research talent in business enterprise is defined as the share of professionals engaged in the concept or creation of new knowledge, products, processes, methods and systems, as well as in the management of these projects. The US have a high score with regard to research talent in business enterprise, and also in relation to high tech imports, but receive a less positive judgment as FDI net inflows (weak point) and ICT services imports are concerned. Foreign Direct Investments are investments from abroad which affect economic growth by increasing total investments in the host country, but also have a positive impact on total factor productivity in that country.[48] Factors that influence FDI are market growth, currency fluctuations, government incentives, relative wage rates, political stability etc. In spite of the strong points of the US, investments from abroad (expressed as a % of GDP) are modest. Perhaps one of the reasons is that there are better alternatives for foreign investors in other (emerging) economies in Asia and Eastern Europe. The US have a better achievement regarding intellectual property payments (% total trade) because it belongs to the top 20 countries.

Due to the strong performance for a number of indicators the US rank 8 in the field of **business sophistication.** But countries like Singapore,

---

[47] Source : Unesco

[48] See: Determinants of economic growth in the United States : the role of Foreign Direct Investments. (Parviz Ashegian, 2010)

Sweden and Switzerland have a higher score. The difference with the top country (Singapore) is 9 points. The next pillar is **knowledge and technology outputs.**

Knowledge and technology outputs depend on *knowledge creation, knowledge impact and knowledge diffusion. Knowledge creation* is related to the number of patents filed at a national or regional patent office per billion GDP (PPP), the number of international patent applications filed by residents at the Patent Cooperation Treaty per billion GDP (PPP), the number of scientific and technical articles per billion GDP (PPP), the economy's number of published articles (H),that have received at least H citations. The latter gives a quantification of both journal scientific productivity and scientific impact.[49] With respect to *knowledge creation* the US belong to the top ten countries in the world. The difference in scores with Switzerland (the top country) is not so big. The US are a very strong country when citable documents are concerned and has also a high score also regarding the number of national patents. The country is a top 15 country regarding international patents, but is less successful in the field of scientific and technical articles (per billion GDP PPP). *Knowledge impact* depends on the growth rate of GDP per worker (%), computer software spending (% GDP), quality management systems (the number of ISO 9001 quality certificates per billion GDP) and finally the output share of high and medium high tech manufactures. The US rank 3 when *knowledge impact* is concerned. This high ranking is caused by the computer software spending (% GDP). The performance regarding the growth rate of GDP per worker[50] and the quality management systems is rather weak. In addition the output share of high and medium high tech manufactures in the US ranks only 11 in the world.

Knowledge diffusion is influenced by intellectual property receipts (% total trade), high tech exports less re-exports (% total trade), ICT services exports (% total trade) and foreign direct investments net outflows (%GDP). The US is the top country regarding intellectual property

---

[49] for more information see the description of the H index by Wikipedia

[50] Situation 2016, in this year and in the period 2010-2016 the growth rate of GDP per person engaged (constant 2011 PPP$) of the US lagged somewhat behind that of the advanced economies. However in the period 1995-2010 productivity growth of the US was somewhat higher than the growth rate of the advanced economies (see also table 8)

receipts (% total trade), but has a weak performance with regard to ICT services exports and is far from a top ten country with respect to high tech exports and Foreign Direct Investments (net outflows). US investments in foreign countries can be beneficial for US enterprises because they can benefit from relative low wage rates, favorable market conditions, avoid trade barriers like tariffs and quota's etc. For the US economy as a whole outward investment can lead to increased overseas investment income (profits from overseas subsidiaries, dividends from owning shares in overseas firms, interest payments from lending abroad) and productivity increase.[51] As a result of the achievements mentioned above there is a large difference between the scores of Switzerland and the US with respect to *knowledge diffusion.*

Consequently the US lag 19,3 points behind Switzerland in the case of **knowledge and technology outputs.** The last pillar is **creative outputs.** Creative outputs depend on *intangible assets, creative goods and services* and *online creativity. Intangible assets* are related to trademarks by origin per billion GDP(PPP), industrial design by origin per billion GDP (PPP), ICT' s and business creation, ICT's and organizational model creation. Trademarks by origin refers to the number of trademark applications issued to residents at a national or regional office (per billion GDP). Industrial design by origin stands for the number of designs contained in industrial design applications filed at a given national or regional office. ICT's and business creation deals with the question to what extent do ICT's enable new business models, whereas ICT's and organizational model creation answers the question to what extent do ICT's enable new organizational models (virtual teams, remote working, telecommuting). For ICT's and organizational model creation the US is the top country. This means that ICT's have created new organizations within enterprises and government on a large scale. On the other hand the US have a weak performance in relation to the number of trademarks by origin. This is also the case with industrial design by origin. In the case of ICT's and business model creation the US have a better score and belongs to the top ten countries in the world. With regard to total *intangible assets* the US lag considerably behind the top country (Switzerland).

Creative goods and services are influenced by cultural and services exports (% of total trade), the number of national feature films produced

---

[51] See : Economics Online, Global Economics, Foreign Direct Investments, 2019

(per million population of 15-69 years), the relative position on the global entertainment and media market (per 1000 population of 15-69 years), printing and publishing manufactures output (% total output)) and the exports of creative goods (% total trade).

The US are the top country as far as cultural and creative services exports are concerned. The country also has a top ranking on the global entertainment and media market. However with respect to the number of national feature films, the share of printing and publishing output and creative goods exports the US are considerably less successful. The last sub pillar is *online creativity*. *Online creativity* is determined by the total number of registered top level domains per thousand population of 15-69 years, country code top level domains per thousand population of 15-69 years[52], Wikipedia yearly edits per million population of 15-69 years and mobile app creation per billion GDP (ppp). Generic top level domains and country code top level domains and country code top level domains belong to the information economy, which in turn influences the knowledge economy.

The US are the top country regarding the number of generic top level domains (TLD) in thousand of population 15-69. For the number of registered country code domains in thousand population 15-69 and Wikipedia edits /million population 15-69 the performance of the US is considerably weaker. For mobile app creation in billion GDP (PPP) the US succeed in getting the 14th place.

For the pillar **creative outputs** as a whole Switzerland (the top country) has a quite higher score than the US (11,4 points), which is caused by some weak achievements of the US with regard to some sub pillars: trademarks by origin/billion PPP$GDP, industrial designs by origin/billion PPP$GDP, country code

Top Level Domains (TLD)/thousand population 15-69.

In table 11 the strong and weak points of the US according to the GII are mentioned.

---

[52] These domains have been determined by the Internet Assigned Numbers Authority (IANA) for use in the internet.

Table 11: Strong and weak points for innovation in the US

Strong Points	Weak Points
Cost of redundancy dismissal	Pisa scales in reading, maths and science *
Ease of resolving insolvency	Pupil-teacher ratio, secondary
Average expenditure R&D top 3 global companies by R&D (million $)	Graduates science and engineering
QS university ranking, average score top 3 universities	Gross capital formation, % GDP
Ease of getting credit	GDP/ unit of energy use
Domestic credit to private sector, %GDP	ISO 14001 environmental certificates/ billion GDP (PPP)
Venture capital deals /billion GDP (ppp)	GERD financed by abroad
Intensity of local competition **	FDI net inflows, % GDP
Domestic market scale billion $PPP	Scientific and technical articles /billion GDP (PPP) *
University/industry research collaboration	Growth rate of GDP (PPP)/ worker, %
State of cluster development	ISO 9001 quality certificates/billion GDP (PPP)
High tech net imports, % total trade **	FDI net inflows, % GDP *
Research talent, % in business enterprise **	Trademarks by origin/billion GDP (PPP)
Patent applications by origin/ billion GDP(PPP) **	Intangible assets *
Citable documents H index	Country code TLD/thousand pop 15-60 *
Computer software spending, % GDP	Wikipedia edits/ million pop 15-69 *
Intellectual property receipts, % total trade	
ICT and organizational model creation	
Cultural and creative services exports., % total trade	
Entertainment and media market/ thousand pop 15-69	
Generic top level domains/thousand pop 15-69	

**=a strength relative to the other top 25 ranked GII countries, *=weakness relative to the other top 25

Strong points belong to indicators for which the US rank 1-3, indicators with a rank of 60 and higher are defined as weak points. Factors with a rank of between 26 and 60 can be described as mediocre points. Also a distinction is made between a strength relative to the other 25 ranked GII economies and a weakness relative to the other top 25. Mediocre points are political stability and safety, ease of starting a business, tertiary inbound mobility, ICT services imports (% total trade), ICT services exports (% total trade), industrial design by origin/billion GDP, national feature films/million pop 15-69, country code top level domains/thousand pop 15-69 years and Wikipedia edits/million pop 15-69 years.[53] Thanks to the strong points the US rank 6 on the Global Innovation Index. However due to the weak and mediocre points the US lag behind top countries with respect to almost every pillar in the GII. In table 10 the GII of the US would increase by 12,5 points if it would achieve the same results by pillar as the top countries. This would mean a higher productivity and GDP, as there is a positive relation between the GII and GDP per capita. This will be illustrated below.

$$GDPC = 1,46*INNI -30,95$$

$$(20,0) \qquad (-9,81)$$

$$R^2 = 0,952$$

$$DW = 2,05$$

GDPC = gross domestic product per capita (1000$ nominal) by country for 2018 INNI= innovation scores by country R^2 measures the success of the regression in predicting the values of the dependent variable within the sample. R^2 is one if the regression fits perfectly and zero if it fits no better than the simple mean of the dependent variable. The value of the R^2 indicates that the equation is quite successful in predicting the values of the dependent variable (GDP per capita). As already discussed the Durbin Watson statistic (DW) is a formal test for serial correlation of the residuals, which makes the results unreliable. On the basis of the statistic the hypothesis of serial correlation can be rejected. The values between

---

[53] Country code top level domains and Wikipedia edits are considered a weakness relative to the other top 25 ranked GII countries.

brackets in the equation are the t values of the coefficients and constant term. The t values of the coefficient of INNI and the constant term are higher than 2 which means that the hypothesis that the variables do not belong in the regression must be rejected. The equation means that 1 point additional score on the GII has an effect of $1460 on GDP per capita. If the US would achieve a top position on all the pillars of the GII this would mean an additional score of 12,5 points on the GII (72,3-59,8,see table 12) or 12,5 * $1460 =$18300 additional GDP per capita. As a result an additional growth of about 29 % per capita would occur.[54] Such a result would be achieved with an average score of 77,4 for the input pillars and 67,2 for the output pillars. So the US must increase its score for the input pillars with 9,6 points and for the output pillars with 15,4 points (see also table 12). This implicates an improvement of the inputs in combination with a rise in the efficiency ratio (the ratio of the average score of the output pillars and the average score of the input pillars) from 0,76 to 0,87. The efficiency ratio is an indication of how efficient inputs in the innovation process can be transformed into outputs. In some developed countries like Germany, the Netherlands, Sweden and Switzerland the efficiency ratio is higher than in the US.

Table 12: Scores By Type Of Pillar In Three Cases

	Central variant	Top position	Higher efficiency ratio in central variant
Input pillars	67,8	77,4	67,8
Output pillars	51,8	67,2	65,4
Total scores	59,8	72,3	66,6
Efficiency ratio	0,76	0,87	0,96

Table 12 shows that in case of an increase of the efficiency ratio to 0,96 [55]and keeping the scores of the input pillars constant, the impact on GDP per capita would be 6,8 points or 16 %. How to improve the efficiency ratio in the US falls beyond the scope of this document as well as how to increase the scores of input and output pillars. More research needs

---

[54] Taking into account a nominal GDP per capita of $ 62152 in 2018 (IMF figure)

[55] The efficiency ratio of Switzerland.

to be done. In the next chapter some general policy recommendations will be made to boost the economic development.

Graph 9 GDP per capita in $ (GDPC) and calculated
GDP per capita by country (GDPCC)

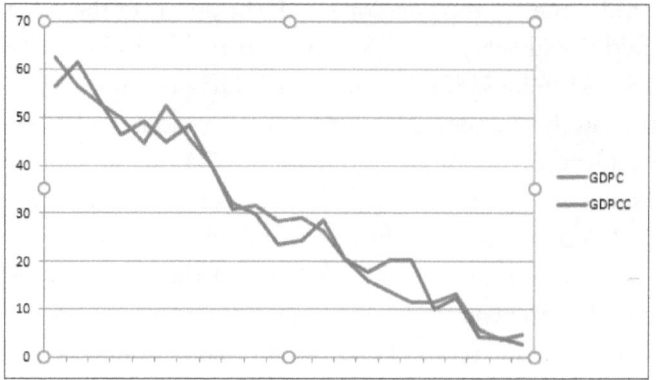

The message from the GII is clear: to improve productivity it is necessary increase the scores of the input pillars and raise the innovation efficiency ratio. However this is rather an abstract message and is not directly useful for policy making. Therefore we will develop some concrete policy options to improve economic performance in the next chapter.

8 POLICY OPTIONS TO
IMPROVE ECONOMIC
PERFORMANCE

8A Stimulating investments by lowering taxes and increasing net profits

An important conclusion from the GII is that in order to increase productivity investments must be stimulated. Investments can introduce embodied technical progress and in this way encourage productivity. Investments can be divided into investments in fixed assets and R&D. For investments in fixed assets and R&D of enterprises a simple model can be assumed : companies pursue a strategy of proportional investments to their sales (%), unless a determinant changes. Determinants are lagged net profits to sales ratio (%), the debt/assets ratio (%) and other variables. If profits increase then the company has more possibilities to invest, a drop in the debt/assets ratio leads to a rise in investments later on. This can be explained by the fact that a company takes risks sooner if it has more risk taking capital at its disposal. A low debt/assets ratio reflects its abilities to bear risks. Moreover a higher debt/assets ratio coincides with a low capacity to bear risks. The model was estimated with data during 1977-1995 from big multinational companies and later aggregated to a number of branches: electronics, computers, software, instruments, drugs, food/soap, chemicals. [56] From this estimation it turned out that a drop in

---

[56] B.Minne : International battle of giants, Central Planning Bureau, the

the debt/assets ratio of 1% point leads to a rise of 0,02 -0,37 % point of the investment (fixed assets) to sales ratio in the year thereafter. If the net profit to sales ratio increases by 1 % point, the investment (fixed assets) to sales ratio increases with 0,02-0,77 % point after one year.

Another category of investments consists of investments in R&D. These investments are meant to create new products or processes and amounted to 2,8 % of GDP in 2017, which is slightly higher than the situation in 2014.[57] Maintaining or increasing the country's R&D efforts is essential if we are to increase the rate of productivity growth and improve American living standards. In 2017 more than 70 % of these expenditures was paid by enterprises, mainly by big multinational companies.[58] In the US tech companies like Amazon, Alphabet, Intel, Microsoft and Apple are the top companies in R&D spending. If we apply the same model for investments in R&D as for investments in fixed assets, the same determinants for investments in R&D can be found, namely the debt/assets ratio and the net profits to sale ratio. A drop in the debt assets ratio of 1 % point means a rise in the R&D investments to sale ratio of 0-0,32 % point after two years. A rise of 1 % point in the net profits to sale ratio will increase the investments to sale ratio by 0-0,11 % point after two years.

Governments can influence investments of enterprises by creating a favorable investment climate. Instruments are fiscal policy, subsidies, education, infrastructure, stable political environment etc. For investments in R&D policies regarding intellectual property rights, legal responsibility and new standards are important. The new tax bill of the US reduces the tax rate for enterprises from 35 % to 21 %. This reduction makes the US more competitive than before. The old tax rate was the highest in the OECD, the new rate puts the US in the middle of the OECD. However very few businesses in the US paid the top rate, as a result of a lot of loopholes. Nevertheless there will be some tax advantage for enterprises in general. As a result net profits will increase and will stimulate investments. The new bill also switches the US to a territorial system, which means that multinationals will no longer pay US tax on profits from overseas with some exceptions. Companies have stashed a lot of profits abroad to defer taxation in the US. For these cases the US will impose a one-time ultra

Netherlands, June 1997

[57] The situation in 2014 was used in the GIII.

[58] Data OECD

low tax on those profits, 8 % on illiquid assets and 15,5 % on liquid assets like cash. This could bring overseas profits back to the US. The question is only in what way these profits will be spend: on investments, but also on paying down debts, stock buybacks and extra dividends to shareholders. If there is a decrease in the debt/asset ratio due to the paying down of debts this could lead to more investments after some time. The new tax bill also reduces the top rate from 39,6 % to 37 % paid by individuals making more than $500000 a year and married households making more than $600000. The other brackets are also slightly lower and they kick in at new income amounts. About 80 % of American taxpayers will pay less taxes this year. However the tax reduction is temporary and ends in 2025. In the short term the tax reduction will have a positive impact on domestic sales and therefore on investments. In the long run these effects will decrease and ultimately disappear. Some economists expect a modest increase of investments and a boost of GDP by 3-5 % in a period of 10 years, higher employment and higher wages. Other economist are more pessimistic and project hardly an increase at all. Their argument is that the tax cuts will swell the deficit -even after accounting for added revenue from their effect on economic growth. This could lead to higher interest rates discouraging business to borrow and investment. All in all the tax reduction can trigger some domestic investments, jobs and economic growth. It is also possible that the competitiveness of the US will increase and more foreign investors will invest in the US. However for a real boost in the economy some adjustments will be necessary. These improvements are of a long term nature and can be derived by comparing the scores of the US for each pillar with those of the top country in table 10. Although the scores of the US in the GII are generally satisfactory, in some areas improvements are desirable.

8B Improving scores regarding institutions

With respect to institutions Singapore has much more political stability & safety, better government effectiveness, a better regulatory quality, higher scores concerning the rule of law. Furthermore it is easier to start a business in Singapore. One of the reasons for the lower score of the political stability and safety is the inequality in the country.

8C Reducing inequality by improving primary and secondary education

The inequality is also visible in education. Fewer than half of the children from low -income families go to preschool, so they enter kindergarten lacking the vocabulary, number skills and socializing experiences that children from better-off family possess. When they are in school students from low-income families achieve less well on average and graduate at much lower rates than students from middle-income households. As high school completion is a strong predictor of adult income, this means that students from poor families have less chances of getting a middle income than students from middle class families. Although in the past many attempts has been made to reduce the education gap between poor and non poor students still exists. Students from low income families, students of color, English learners and immigrant students in high poverty neighborhoods are likely to be taught by inexperienced and ineffective teachers in overcrowded schools, which lack adequate means to improve education. Twenty three percent or 16 million American children live in poverty and children of color are more than twice as likely as their white counterparts to be poor. In neighborhoods with higher and middle income households the students are better served. This situation has an impact on the overall quality of education. While 80 percent of high school seniors receive a diploma, less than half of those are able to proficiently read or complete mathematical problems. The OECD develops an international survey (PISA) that examines 15-year-old students' performance in reading, mathematics and science. The US rank only 29 in the world. Expenditure on education are relatively modest in the US. For government expenditure per pupil of secondary schools expressed as a percentage of GDP per capita the US occupy the 41st place. Total expenditure on education in percentage of GDP is 4,9, which means a 54th place in the world. Because part of the education system is failing, fewer than 40 percent of graduating seniors of high school have mastered reading and mathematics and are poorly equipped for college and real world life. These students are at a serious disadvantage and have an increased chance of falling behind and dropping out of college. The US lag well behind many other advanced nations with respect to student knowledge and skills. This can be harmful for the competitiveness of the American economy.

There is a possibility that people that attend urban high schools but do not earn a diploma are lost to the school to prison pipeline. A high crime rate can affect the stability and safety of the country. It is therefore essential to improve the achievements of the educational system. To promote a better and more equitable education system there are three important factors which must be recognized :[59]

- A foundational focus on improving the overall quality of schools and school systems by means of a coherent, standards-based approach coupled with continuous improvement processes at all levels of the system.
- High leverage targeted strategies adapted to local environments to address issues particularly consequential for traditionally underserved students.
- Effective connections among schools and other institutions and organizations touching students lives.

This means the formulation of challenging standards stating what students should know and be able to succeed at different points in their schooling and afterwards. Furthermore policies which aim at building capacity and ensure that all students have access to opportunities to meet those standards. Also a governance system which is characterized by a broad central direction in combination with local discretion, knowledge and innovation to achieve the goals for students.

A continuous improvement approach is necessary. Apart from rising the quality of the standards that guide instruction and supportive policy lessons should be learned from successes and failures of the past. In addition four targeted strategies should be applied to reduce inequalities. - Creating safe and supportive school environments Safety and support can stimulate child and parent to establish a social emotional learning culture, which is necessary for a student to be successful. - Developing language Language skills are important for a child during his while school period.

Children from poor families often have little access to preschool opportunities and English learners language development may be essential for their success in later grades. Therefore they need special help acquiring the literacy and oral language skills. For students whose families don't speak English at home this is a real challenge.

---

[59] This section was derived from :: Equality and quality in US education, American Institute for Research, Education Policy Center, September 2016

- Implementing tiered interventions First there must be a high quality, accessible core instruction program for all students (tier 1), followed by appropriate interventions for students who encounter difficulty succeeding in that program (tiers 2 and 3). Tier 2 interventions could include tutoring by a reading specialist and other intensive customized help. Tier 3 is relevant for the 5-10 % of students who still don't respond. For them special services could be needed or even an individualized education program.

- Pay attention to student transition points Transition points are predictable points in the career of a student through school, which can be consequential for later success, especially for students from low income families. Important transition points are the schooling in Kindergarten, the intermediate grades (between grades 3 and 4), transition to middle school, transition through high school. In high school early warning systems, multiple pathways and strong counseling can help that all students graduate and have the necessary performance and course prerequisites to pursue postsecondary opportunities. However not only schools are important for students to succeed. Good medical care, healthy food, a supportive and language –rich environment, recreational facilities and access to preschool are among the conditions that poor neighborhoods lack and that other organizations or the government can provide. Connecting schools to such organizations or the government could be fruitful to the development of students from less – advantaged backgrounds. Better schooling can lead to a better preparation for college. A higher quality of schooling for students from low-income neighborhoods can reduce inequality and improve the quality of labor and thus productivity.

8D Improving competitiveness by stimulating STEM at tertiary education

If we l ook at tertiary education the GII regards the graduates of science and engineering in the US (in % of total graduates) as a weak point of the economy. With a percentage of about 14 % the US lag behind a lot of developed and emerging countries. Science, Technology, Engineering and Mathematics (STEM) are important for innovation. Innovation can be defined as the creation of new products, services and new processes. Research and Development (R&D) is often necessary to bring about innovative developments. Workers in the field of R&D have largely a STEM background. So in order to stimulate innovation an adequate number of STEM graduates must be available. Table 13 illustrates the number of STEM graduates (in % of total graduates) for both sexes and females for a number of countries'

Table 13 The number of graduates in STEM by country (% of total graduates) in 2016

Country	Share of total graduates	Share of female graduates
Germany	36,0	19,3
India	31,7	26,9
France	25,6	14,5
Korea	29,9	15,4
Sweden	26,6	15,0
Switzerland	24,5	11,1
UK	26,3	17,5
US	17,9	10,4

Source : UNESCO Institute for Statistics

The US lag behind with regard to STEM education compared to some other developed countries and an emerging economy like India. The low level of STEM education for women in the US is remarkable. Increasing the number of STEM graduates can be realized by encouraging students for whom science and mathematics are their best subjects and who enjoy it but still don't choose it. Especially women must be persuaded by means of mentorships programs for high performing women and recruitment programs at a university graduate level to follow a STEM education. With more people with a STEM background available for the R&D sector the creation of new brands and processes will improve. This will lead to a higher productivity and economic growth.[60] For an analysis of STEM education on economic growth see e.g. Mallory Croak : The effects of STEM Education on Economic Growth, Union College, 2018 and Rita

---

[60] Immigration of persons with a STEM education could also contribute to more economic growth.

Ray :STEM Education and Economic Performance in the American States, MPRA Paper, July 2015.

8E Improving competitiveness by increasing energy productivity

A special case of efficiency growth is the development of energy productivity. Energy productivity can be described as the ratio between GDP and energy consumption in physical units. It shows how much value added is generated by one unit of energy. The level of energy productivity depends on factors like economic structure, climate, energy efficiency and geography. Manufacturing -focused economies tend to have a lower energy productivity (or a higher energy intensity) than service-oriented economies. Countries with wider temperature variations tend to use more energy for heating and cooling. The distance between urban areas and the infrastructure within them can influence the amount of energy used to move goods and passengers. Energy productivity in the US has grown in the period 1990-2015 by 1,9 % per annum. In OECD countries and in the world as a whole energy productivity increased by 1,5 %. A part of these productivity gains was due to structural shifts in the economy, another part was due to efficiency gains. These improvements can be triggered by higher energy prices, making energy conservation more attractive, government policies such as subsidies, regulations, standards and technological developments caused by R&D.

For future developments we can look at the International Energy Outlook of the EIA, which gives projections of energy use and production for the US, the OECD and the rest of the world till 2040. For our purpose the reference scenario and the period 2015-2025 are considered. The reference scenario contains the views of leading economic forecasters and demographers related to economic and demographic trends. In the projections current laws, regulations and stated targets are taken into account. An important variable for energy demand is economic growth. In the reference scenario a volume growth of GDP of 2,3 % per annum during 2015-2025 is estimated for the US, for the OECD and the world a volume growth of GDP (in PPP) is projected of 1,8 % resp. 3,3 % per annum for the same period. The price of crude oil in this scenario rises from $ 52 per barrel for Brent oil and $49 per barrel for WTI oil in 2015 to $ 77 per barrel (Brent) and $74 per barrel (WTI) for 2025.[61]

Table 14 GDP (PPP) in prices of 2015 (billion $)

	2015	2020	2025	Av. growth Per annum 2015-2025
US	18219	20262	22842	2,3
OECD	52920	57814	63546	1,8
World	115729	136101	159983	3,3

Source : EIA

Table 15 Energy demand (million toe)

	2015	2020	2025	Av. growth Per annum 2015-2025
US	2227	2289	2300	0,3
OECD	5495	5589	5676	0,3
World	13060	13729	14410	1,0

Source : EIA

Table 16 Energy productivity

	2015	2020	2025	Av. growth Per annum 2015-2025
US	8,181	8,85	9,93	2,0
OECD	9,63	10,34	11,20	1,5
World	8,86	9,91	11,10	2,3

Source : EIA

Economic growth in the US is estimated to be 2,3 % per annum for the period 2015-2025, whereas average GDP growth in the OECD is projected 0,5 % point lower. For the world as a whole an annual expansion of GDP is estimated of 3,3 %. Energy demand in the next 10 years however

---

[61] In prices of 2015

increases at a modest rate in the US and OECD, but also in the world as a whole due to the increase of energy productivity. Energy productivity rises as a result of efficiency improvement and shifts in the economic structure from energy intensive to less energy intensive activities. The level of energy productivity in the US in 2015 lagged 15 % behind that of the OECD and is 8 % lower than the energy productivity in the world as a whole. In 2025 the ratio of GDP per unit of energy in the US is still 12 % lower than in the OECD and 11 % lower than in the world as a whole. Fossil fuels still dominate in the next 10 years, but there is some shift to renewable energy (see graph 10). Oil consumption declines after 2020 mainly due to continuing efficiency improvement in the transport sector, the main consumption category for oil. World oil prices rise in real terms and influence the prices of gasoline and diesel and thus also the demand for oil products in this scenario. Oil production is projected to recover from the production dip after the oil price crash, as a result of the assumed oil price increase in the projection period in combination with cost reductions. The US however remain a net importer of oil during the next ten years, but the dependence of foreign oil decreases. Natural gas consumption is influenced by natural gas prices, which in turn are related to the development of US natural gas resources. Since 2005 gas prices have decreased due to more efficiency with regard to the production of natural gas from shale and tight formations, stimulating domestic demand and net exports. After 2020 the price of gas rises slowly due to production expansion into less prolific and more expensive to produce areas. This development has a small negative impact on the demand growth of natural gas. Other factors which are important for the consumption of gas are regulations and incentives with regard to fuels and technologies that compete with electricity generation fueled by natural gas. Efficiency standards for buildings, furnaces and other appliances also have an impact on the demand for natural gas (and electricity). Production of natural gas rises during 2015-2025 but the rate of growth decreases after 2020. The US becomes a net exporter of natural gas. Coal consumption declines considerably as a result of the assumed lower input in the electricity plants. This development however depends on the policy regulations regarding the input of energy in the electricity sector. The Clean Power Plan of former president Obama comprised a cut of 32 percent of carbon dioxide emissions below 2005 levels, a target that was central to the commitment of the United States to reduce green house gas emissions under the 2015 Paris Climate Agreement. This Clean Power

Plan implied a large reduction of coal in the electricity sector due to the relatively large CO_2 emission of coal. President Trump has withdrawn the US from the Paris agreement and has started a process for replacing the Clean Power Plan. So there are large uncertainties with regard to the future consumption of coal. In the reference scenario it is assumed that unfavorable economic conditions compared with natural gas and renewable energy result in a declining coal fired generation. Coal production decreases in accordance with lower demand for coal.

Graph 10 Shares of energy carriers 2015-2025

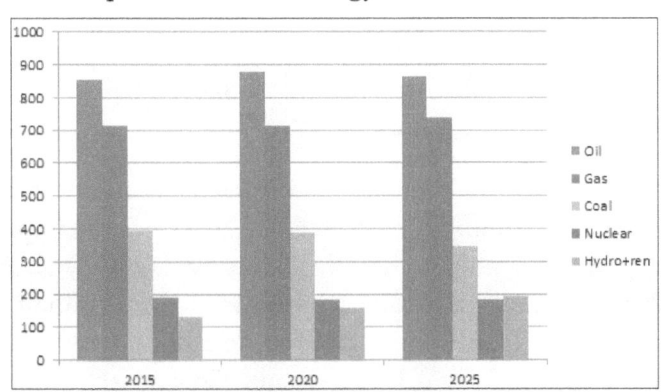

Nuclear energy demand remains stable till 2025, because no new nuclear capacity is built during this period. The combination of low natural gas prices, higher renewable penetration, low electricity load growth and relatively high capital cost hampers a extension of nuclear capacity. Wind and solar generation become the predominant sources of renewable generation in the coming 10 years, whereas hydro energy production remains stable after 2020. Substantial cost reductions, performance improvements and a permanent 10% investment tax credit support solar generation. Many wind projects are economic without a tax credit. Most of the profitable wind projects however are constructed to take advantage of the tax credit prior to their planned expiration. Due to these developments renewable energy increases at a fast rate. The rise of energy productivity has a favorable impact on energy costs for energy consumers and emissions of NOX, SO2 and CO_2. As a result of rising energy productivity and the shift to renewable energy CO_2 emissions decrease from 5248 kton in 2015 to 5057 kton in 2025. As a result of higher energy productivity, higher domestic oil and gas production and a higher penetration of renewable energy the deficit on the balance of payment will decrease during the next ten years.

Table17 Oil and gas production, consumption and balance 2015-2025 (million tons of oil equivalent)

	2015	2020	2025
Oil prod	565	627	649
Oil cons	898	926	912
Balance	-333	-299	-263
Gas prod	637	726	780
Gas cons	639	639	660
Balance	-2	87	120

In physical terms the improvement of the balance of payment for oil can be calculated as 70 million toe (=263-333), for gas the impact on the balance of payment amounts to 122 million toe (120+2). Expressed in prices of 2015 this means a reduction of the deficit by 40 billion dollars or 8 % of the total deficit in 2015 (500 billion dollars).

The study of ACEEE (35 Years and Counting)[62] indicates that there are ample possibilities to increase energy productivity during the next 35 years. An improvement of more than 3 % per annum could be realized during this period, about 1 % point more than in the reference scenario. With regard of efficiency gains the following opportunities can be distinguished:

– Better systems integration, among others intelligent efficiency. This means the use of sensors, controls, big data and computer chips to monitor and control energy use in real time.
– Improvement of many types of equipment (such as computers, televisions and elevators)
– Evolution of building design to yield zero net energy and ultra low energy buildings.
– Energy process improvements.

[62] American Council for an Energy Efficient Economy: 35 years and counting, June 2015

- Increased use of advanced vehicles including electric, hybrid and self driving vehicles
- Improve building energy retrofits to a higher level in order to obtain larger savings per building
- Better efficiency of the electric grid by means of additional heat and power systems, greater power plant efficiency, reduced transmission and distribution losses, expanded use of other distribution generation resources and improved grid control and integration.
- Promotion of sustainable development and transportation patterns.
- Initiatives to change wasteful energy-using behaviors among consumers and businesses

In order to realize the ambitious efficiency goals mentioned above it will be necessary to support and sometimes transform markets to boost demand for efficient goods and services.

A possibility to stimulate energy efficiency is to inform consumers about the options and related costs of energy conservation. Government and other organizations Labeling the energy use of appliances and other types of equipment can be useful for consumers to make the right decisions. The same goes for the energy use of buildings and homes, which could be applied by cities or states. Building codes or equipment efficiency standards have also been very useful in the past and must be continued. Such a policy of the government can also trigger new, even more efficient technologies and practices. Research and Development with respect of new energy -savings technologies and practices can enlarge the market of energy efficiency options and reduce the limitations of existing technologies and practices. Furthermore easy to access financing is a tool for stimulating energy efficiency investments among consumers and businesses that are capital constrained. This type of financing can be applied by governments (green banks) or firms and organizations (standard financing packages). A further refinement and additional creative new mechanisms will be useful to increase energy efficiency.

Utilities can play an important role with regard to energy efficiency by delivering energy efficiency services to their clients. It will be necessary however to change their business model, because their sales will be negatively affected by energy conservation. Also the increasing popularity of distributed generation will slow down the growth in the deliveries of utilities to energy consumers. Their business model should embrace efficiency efforts. Energy rates which depend on the time of use [63]can also promote energy efficiency. Government is also an important player regarding the promotion of energy efficiency. In the past standards with respect to appliances, equipment and building codes have been successful. Also policies promoting energy efficiency investments of utilities had quite an impact. Municipalities have also started to improve their energy efficiency, helped by energy efficiency block grants. The federal government had an important role with regard to energy efficiency R&D (Energy Star) and efficiency standards for appliances and vehicles.

All these measures from the past should be continued and, if possible, intensified to achieve an increase of energy productivity of 3 % per annum. Additional support for the development of renewables[64] can reduce the use of fossil fuels, promote energy security and improve the environment. If as a result of extra efforts the use of gas and oil would reduce by another 10 % and domestic production would remain on the level of the reference scenario, then the deficit of the oil balance would decrease by 87 million toe, whereas the surplus on the gas balance would surge by 64 million toe. In prices of 2015 this would mean a reduction of the balance of payment deficit of 38 billion dollars or 8 % of the total deficit in 2015.

8F Agencies can play an important part in the knowledge economy

Agencies can contribute to innovation by accelerating technological change. Their contribution consists of : identification of promising areas of new technology, funding research, creating a network of stakeholders in the innovation process (big and small firms, university and government laboratories), linking university researchers to entrepreneurs interested in starting a new firm, connecting start-up firms with venture capitalists, supporting the commercialization process in finding a large firm which can bring the new product to the market or assisting in procuring a government contract. In this way research projects with a risky character and a long term focus can be realized. Risky research is not popular with the private sector. Moreover this sector is used to invest in developing

---

[63] In this way we can distinguish base load rates, middle load rates and peak load rates.

[64] Among others the improvement of battery technology for electric cars, the promotion of investment cost reductions.

---

cost competitive products in a limited time horizon (the 3 to 5 year time frame). An important agency is The Defense Advanced Research Agency (DARPA), which has helped to develop technologies such as computers, jet planes, civilian nuclear energy, lasers and biotechnology.

9 Summary

The US economy grew at a modest rate of 1,8 % per annum during 2000 2016. There were differences of production growth by sector with a less than average activity increase in industry, construction, wholesale, public administration and other services. Sectors with a more than average value added growth were the agricultural sector, information and communication, professional services and real estate. Due to the modest economic growth and an increase in labor productivity of 1,2 % per annum total employment rose by 0,6 % per annum. In the reference period there was a shift in the composition of employment from lower levels of education (less than high school, high school graduates) to the highest level (bachelors degree and higher). As a result of demographic developments the share of older people increased at the cost of young and prime aged people. Labor force growth (0,7 % per annum) was tempered by the decrease of the participation rate for the population of 16 years and older. This drop can be ascribed to increased schooling, aging of the population (retirement), poor health and / or disability and the discouraged workers effect. Unemployment rose from 4 % of the total labor force in 2000 to 9,6 % in the period 2008-2010 and dropped to 4,9 % in 2016. However this figure could be an underestimation of the "real" unemployment as a result of the discouraged worker effect. Unemployment rates in 2016 vary by level of education. The higher the education level the lower the unemployment rate. The unemployment rate of people with level 1 (less than high school) education is three times as high as the unemployment rate of people with level 4 education (bachelors degree and higher). People with level 2 education (high school graduates) have an unemployment rate which is twice as high as the unemployment rate of people with level 4 education. Due to the weak demand for labor the real average wage rate grew by 0,6 % per annum, which was lower than the increase of labor productivity. As a result the share of labor compensation in total GDP declined. However there were differences between categories of labor. The top tenth of the distribution received a real wage increase which was five times higher than those of the bottom tenth.

During the reference period there has been a loss of market share on the domestic and international market. On the domestic market this loss was caused by unfavorable relative prices. Relative prices are not only related to unfavorable cost price developments in the US, but could also have been influenced by currency manipulation or subsidies by the exporting foreign country.

On the international market the loss of market share can be partly explained by the development of the investment ratio of the US which lags behind the growth of the average investment ratio of the main competitors. This ratio is an indicator of the introduction of new products and services. Also relative prices could have played some part. However exports have also been influenced by the degree of openness of the importing countries, foreign subsidies and currency manipulation. These developments had a negative impact on economic growth (especially on the production of manufactures),employment, government budget and balance of payment. Economic performance can be improved by investing in skills, promoting a level playing field with foreign countries and winning the race by a robust innovation system.

Investing in skills is necessary because the US lag behind other OECD countries regarding proficiency in numeracy and to a lesser extent also with regard to proficiency in numeracy. Better skills can attract more economic activity concerning products and services with a high value added. A level playing field is essential for all countries involved to benefit from free trade agreements. In practice however countries (especially China) try to export as much as possible and import as less as possible by cheating the WTO rules and other agreements. Recently the US has concluded trade agreements with Canada and Mexico to improve a level playing field with those countries. Taxation of imported Chinese goods in the US was intended to stimulate further talks on trade with China. Trade agreements to achieve a level playing field can be highly recommended. Creating a robust innovation system is essential to maintain or even improve competitiveness of the US economy. The GII describes the innovative capacity of countries by giving scores for each country regarding 7 pillars, divided into sub pillars and variables. The higher the total score, the higher the (potential) GDP per capita. The US rank 6 on 127 countries. From this survey a list of strong points, weak points and mediocre points can be distinguished for the US economy. Due to the weak and mediocre points the US lag behind some other developed countries with regard to every pillar of the GII except for market sophistication where the US is the top country. A partial and static approach can be made to calculate the impact on economic growth if the US would have the same score as the top country for each pillar.

In the field of **institutions** the US rank 13 due to the mediocre score regarding political stability and safety as well as for the ease of starting a business. This has a negative impact on productivity and economic growth. From several international studies it can be proven that political instability reduces productivity and economic growth.[65] The difference in scores with Singapore is 7 points or 1,6 % in terms of GDP per capita.[66]

With regard to **human capital and research** the US present a mixed picture. On the one hand the US top 3 universities rank nr 1 in the world and the average expenditure on R&D of the top 4 global companies is the world's highest, on the other hand there are some weak points in the educational system. These weak points have a negative impact on productivity and competitiveness of the economy. There is an education gap between poor and non poor students. Students from low income families achieve less well on average and graduate at much lower rates than students from middle-income families. In poor neighborhoods the quality (and safety) of the schooling system lags behind that of higher and middle income quarters. This means that students from poor families has less chances of getting a middle income than students from middle class families as high school completion is a strong predictor of adult income. While 80 % of high school seniors receive a diploma, less than half of those are able to proficiently read and compete mathematical problems. So they are poorly equipped for college and real life. In the PISA survey the US only rank 29 in the world due to insufficient skills of the students.

---

[65] See e.g. A.Aisen and F.Veiga : How does political instability affect economic growth? IMF working paper, 2011

[66] 7 points mean 0,7 points for the average total score of the GII, which generates 1,46*0,7=1,022 additional GDP per capita or 1,6 % taking into account a GDP/cap of 62152 dollar in 2018. See also chapter 7C

To improve and to promote a more equitable educational system three important strategies should be adopted:

1. A foundational focus on improving the overall quality of schools and school systems by means of a coherent, standards based approach coupled with continuous improvement processes of all levels of the system.
2. High leverage targeted strategies adapted to local environments to address issues particularly consequential for traditionally underserved students.
3. Effective connections among schools and other institutions and organizations touching students lives.

In order to promote innovation an adequate number of graduates in the field of Science, Technology , Engineering and Mathematics (STEM) is necessary. The US lags behind with regard to STEM education compared with some other developed countries and an emerging economy like India. Especially the low level of STEM education of women is remarkable. Students with the right skills could be encouraged to join a STEM education. Especially high performing women must be persuaded by means of mentorships programs and recruitment programs. If the US would have the same score of the top country (Singapore) it would have 22 points more, which means an increase in GDP per capita of 5,2 %.[67]

The US rank 24 in the field of **infrastructure,** which is the result of a top ten position for ICT, a less prominent position for general infrastructure and a weak achievement regarding ecological sustainability. Improvement of the scores for general infrastructure can be attained by stimulating investments, because the gross capital formation (%GDP) of the US lags behind a lot of other advanced economies. The profit tax reduction of the president is a step in the right direction. The ecological sustainability can be promoted by formulating an environmental policy, which aims at achieving environmental objectives. A cornerstone for the ecological sustainability is the formulation of an energy policy which aims at an increase of energy productivity (the ratio between GDP and the domestic

---

[67] 22 points mean 2,2 points for the average total score of the GII, which generates 1,46*2,2=3,212 additional GDP per capita or 5,2 %, taking into account a GDP/cap of 62152 dollar in 2018

use of energy in physical units). Energy productivity can increase by a shift in production to less energy intensive production and a raise in efficiency. Efficiency gains can be triggered by higher energy prices, government policies and technological developments. The level of energy productivity in the US for 2015 lagged 15 % behind that of the OECD in total, so there is probably room for improvement. According to the International Energy Outlook of the EIA energy demand in the US will only increase by 0,3 % per annum from 2015-2025, taking into account an annual GDP increase of 2,3 % and an oil price which rises from $52 (Brent) in 2015 and $49 (WTI) to $77-$74 per barrel in prices of 2015. This means a growth in energy productivity of 2 % per annum, which is slightly higher than the productivity growth during 1990-2015. The higher energy productivity has a favorable impact on energy costs, the balance of payment and the environment. The environment benefits from an increased penetration of wind and solar energy and a decline in domestic oil consumption and an assumed decrease of coal consumption. The balance of payment improves due to the rising oil and gas production and the stagnating domestic energy consumption. Therefore the deficit decreases in 2015 by 8 % (in prices of 2015). According to the ACEEE the energy productivity could be increased by an additional 1 % per annum. Then the productivity of the US would be about equal to that of the OECD. This can be realized by government policies such as subsidies, regulations and standards. Cooperation with utilities and municipalities can be useful to achieve this ambitious goal. In addition technological developments due to R&D are essential for a boost in energy productivity. As a result the deficit on the balance of payment will decrease further as well as the emissions of CO_2. The top country in the field of **infrastructure** is Hong Kong, which has 10 points more than the US. This difference in scores yields 2,3 % additional economic growth per capita.[68]

The US are the top country with regard to **market sophistication,** which is caused by the favorable situation on the credit market, the high value of market capitalization and venture capital deals, but also by the intensity of local competition and the domestic market scale. Such an achievement contributes to the productivity and competitiveness of the US economy.

---

[68] 10 points mean a contribution of 1 point for the average GII index, which generates 1,46 dollars of GDP per capita or 2,3 %., taking into account a GDP/cap of 62152 dollar in 2018

In the field of **business sophistication** the US are strong regarding university/industry research collaboration, the state of cluster development, the use of research talent in business enterprises and high tech net imports as well as research talent (%) in business enterprises. Gross expenditures performed by business (%GDP) or financed by business (%) do not rank top five, but top ten in the world. Weak points are FDI net inflows (%GDP) and GERD financed by abroad (%). The US score 9 points less than the top country (the Netherlands) which represents an additional GDP per capita of 2,1 %.[69]

Strong points in the field of **knowledge and technology outputs** are the number of patents by origin (billion PPP$ GDP), the number of published articles (H index), computer software spending (%GDP), the number of resident patent applications /billion PPP$ GDP and intellectual property receipts (% total trade).

Weak points are the number of scientific and technical articles /billion PPP$GDP, the quality management and FDI net outflows (%GDP). ICT services exports in terms of total trade are relatively low. Furthermore the growth rate of PPP$GDP/worker in the US lagged a little behind that of the advanced economies in some recent years in the past (2014, 2016,2017)

In spite of the strong points the US score is no less than 19,3 points lower than that of Switzerland, the top country. This difference in scores represents an additional GDP per capita of 11,3.[70]

The last pillar for the innovation index is **creative outputs.**

Strong points for the US are ICT's & organizational model creation, ICT's and business model creation, entertainment and media market /1000 pop 15-69, generic top level domains on the internet/ 1000 pop 15-69 and cultural and creative services exports (% total trade). However there are also some weak points : the number of trademarks by origin/billion PPPGDP, the number of industrial designs by origin/billion PPP GDP, the number of country code top level domains on the internet/1000 pop 15-69, the number of Wikipedia edits/million pop 15-69 and the number

---

[69] 9 points represents 0,9 points for total GII, which generate 0,9*1,46= 1,31 dollars of GDP per capita or 2,1 %.taking into account a GDP/Cap of 62152 dollar in 2018

[70] 19,3 points mean 4,825 points for total GII (=19,3*0,25), which generate 7,04 dollars of GDP per capita (7,04*1,46) or 11,3 %, taking into account a GDP/Cap of 62152 dollar in 2018.

of national feature films produced/million pop 15-69. Compared to the top country (Switzerland) the US score is 11,4 points lower, which generates an additional GDP per capita of 6,7 %. [71]

Analysis of the GII shows that in spite of a lot of strong points there is room for further improvement for innovation in the US. If the US would have a score of the top country for each innovation pillar the total score of the innovation index would rise with 12,5 points, which generates an additional GDP per capita of about 29 %. Some suggestions have been made above to increase the innovation efforts. Increasing the efficiency ratio can also contribute to a higher GDP per capita.

Important topics in the presented analysis were the deficit on the balance of payment, problems on the labor market and the related large differences in wage levels between groups of workers and the relatively low investment to GDP ratio.

These problems can be addressed by the following instruments: educational policy, investment policy, trade policy and policy regarding the energy productivity. Improvement in educational policy regarding secondary and postsecondary education can increase the skills of the US worker, increase their productivity, the competitiveness of the US economy, improve the employability and wage levels of large groups of employees and probably also the balance of payment.

A larger share of STEM graduates will create more new products and services, rise productivity and stimulate exports (of high tech products and services), investments and economic growth. More exports will also reduce the deficit on the balance of payment. In addition to tax incentives and subsidies, government agents like DARPA (Defense Advanced Research Projects Agency) can play an important role in the knowledge economy. Identifying interesting innovative breakthroughs, investing in promising, but risky projects, creating a network of stakeholders of the innovation process has helped to accelerate the technological development.

Stimulating tertiary inbound mobility is a way to tap into a global pool of talent, support the development of innovation and production systems and mitigate the impact of an ageing population on future skills supply.

---

[71] 11,4 points have an impact of 2,85 points for total GII (11,4*0,25), which generate 4,16 dollars of GDP per capita (2,85*1,46) or 6,7 %, taking into account a GDP/Cap of 62152 dollar in 2018.

Investment policy refers to measures that will make capital formation attractive like lower taxes and subsidies. The reduction of profit tax of the present government will probably give a boost to investments in general and generate a rise of expenditures on R&D with favorable effects on productivity and competitiveness. Stimulating Foreign Direct Investments (net inflows) can have a positive impact on economic growth and productivity. This requires policies that are conducive to increasing the amount of Foreign Direct Investments in the US.[72] An adequate trade policy aims at creating a level playing field with foreign competitors. In removing obstacles for free trade US exports can face new opportunities, whereas in combination with a better competitiveness imports can be reduced. This means a decrease of the deficit on the balance of payment A special case of productivity growth is the development of energy productivity. Energy productivity growth can be favorable to the balance of payment. In 2015 energy productivity of the OECD was about 15 % higher than in the US. According to the reference scenario of EIA energy productivity in the US will grow by 2 % per annum till 2025 whereas the OECD will expected to have a productivity growth of 1,5 % per annum. So the productivity gap between the US and the OECD will decrease. As a result of the productivity increase in the US the domestic consumption of oil will hardly grow in the period till 2025 and the domestic consumption of gas will rise at a lower rate than GDP. This means that with a rising oil and gas production the imports of oil can be reduced and the exports of natural gas can flourish. Not only will the balance of payment benefit, but also the environment (e.g. less CO_2 emissions) According to a study of ACEEE an additional increase of energy productivity growth of 1 % per annum can be realized during the next 35 years, which will have an additional positive impact on the balance of payment. Energy productivity gains can occur as a result of structural shifts in the economy to less energy intensive activities and efficiency gains. Efficiency gains can be beneficial for the economy, because they reduce the energy bill for the consumer and the energy costs of the industry.[73] Government policies regarding efficiency improvements consist of subsidies, regulations, standards and the stimulation of R&D.

---

[72] See : Determinants of economic growth in the United States: the role of Foreign Direct Investments by Parviz Asheghian.

[73] Apart from the already mentioned positive impact on the balance of payment.

www.ingramcontent.com/pod-product-compliance
Lightning Source LLC
Chambersburg PA
CBHW021503210526
45463CB00002B/866